"I love Rhonda Rhea's writing a '
mocha — always guaranteed to giv
— PAM FARREL, international spea
  Men Are Like Waffles — Women

"Rhonda Rhea has done it again. *Espresso Your Faith: 30 Shots of God's Word to Keep You Focused on Christ* is just the right balance of humor and insight into God's Word. Watch out! You'll become addicted to Rhonda just like the rest of us."
— MARY ENGLUND MURPHY, author of *Joseph: Beyond the Coat of Many Colors*

"I'd choose a wake-up call from this energizing book anytime! In delightful Rhonda Rhea fashion, *Espresso Your Faith* stirs up a flavorful blend of wit, humor, and spiritual insight that at the same time relaxes and invigorates. Even better than my beloved chai tea lattes, this *Espresso* is a stimulant for the soul!"
— DEBORA M. COTY, award-winning author of *More Beauty, Less Beast*
and *Fear, Faith, and a Fistful of Chocolate*

"*Espresso Your Faith* is filled with wit and wisdom and plenty of solid suggestions for how to maintain our relationship with Jesus, including simple, everyday ways that fit busy lives. I'm a decaf person myself, but after reading this book, I'm ready to switch to *Espresso*."
— KAREN O'CONNOR, author of *It's Taken Years to Get This Old*
and *365 Senior Moments You'd Rather Forget*

"Coffee and humor all wrapped up in God's love! What could be better? I need this book today. So do you — and Rhonda's the one you can trust to serve it up fresh, hearty, and funny!"
— VIRELLE KIDDER, author of *Meet Me at the Well,*
Donkeys Still Talk, The Best Life Ain't Easy, and more

"Is your faith a bit lethargic? Rhonda Rhea's new book will give your faith just the jolt it needs. She has the unique ability to serve up solid biblical truth with a healthy side of caffeinated humor. You will laugh out loud one minute and be ready to respond the next as she challenges you to follow Christ with active alertness."
— KATHY HOWARD, Christian speaker and author of five books,
including *Fed Up with Flat Faith* (New Hope Publishers, March 2013)

"Young or old, married or single, new believer or seasoned Christian, groups or individuals — every woman will benefit from Rhonda's funny, frank, and biblically sound advice in *Espresso*. If you love coffee and want a more robust spiritual life, order an *Espresso* today!"
— NANCY SEBASTIAN MEYER, author of *Talk Easy, Listen Hard: Real*
Communication for Two Really Different People; hope4hearts.net

"*Espresso Your Faith* is a highly caffeinated charge to drink in the Word of God — to let it stir us to live the way we were meant to live."

— GEORGIA SHAFFER, psychologist and author of the best-selling *Taking Out Your Emotional Trash*

"It's true that God uses our passions for His glory — and it so happens Rhonda Rhea's are coffee, caffeine, and comedy! *Espresso Your Faith* serves up a triple shot of laugh-out-loud funny with a hefty dose of humility on the side. Sit down with your favorite cup o' joe and discover God's recipe for refocusing your heart on Jesus Christ."

— JENN DOUCETTE, author of *The Velveteen Mommy* and *Mama Said There'd Be Days Like This*

"From the very beginning, Rhonda Rhea drew me in with her stellar humor and witty observations. I wanted more! (Is that how it is with coffee?) This book provides biblical perspective in a fresh, new way that will delight coffee drinkers and non–coffee drinkers.

— LINDA GILDEN, author of *Mama Was the Queen of Christmas*, *Mommy Pick-Me-Ups* (coauthor), and more

"Every day I need a bit of laughter and caffeine. If you do too, *Espresso Your Faith* is just what the barista ordered. Take a moment to read this book and sip your favorite beverage and your faith will become well-grounded. Rhea shares loads of fun and even more practical, biblical wisdom in this laugh-out-loud charge to be alert to the Lord."

— SUSANNE SCHEPPMANN, author of *Embraced by the Father: Finding Grace in the Names of God*

"*Espresso Your Faith* is a classic example of Rhonda at her best — challenging us right where we live while we hold our sides from laughing. This lady is naturally funny — yet deeply spiritual — and a great writer besides! Don't miss this latest offering from a classy lady."

— KATHI MACIAS (kathimacias.com), author of nearly 40 books, including Golden Scroll 2011 Novel of the Year and Carol Award finalist, *Red Ink*

"If we wouldn't think of starting our day without coffee, why would we attempt it without the soul-charging Word of God? Rhonda Rhea makes it easy to have both. Grab your Bible, a cup of your favorite coffee, and *Espresso Your Faith*. Nothing wakes us up spiritually like an extra shot of God's Word. As we percolate on some of these faith-building charges, we find ourselves waking up to new ways the Lord wants us to grow. What a great way to stay spiritually hot!"

— JOCELYN GREEN, author of *Faith Deployed: Daily Encouragement for Military Wives* and *Faith Deployed . . . Again*

Espresso Your Faith

OTHER NEW HOPE BOOKS BY RHONDA RHEA

*How Many Lightbulbs Does It Take to Change a Person?
Bright Ideas for Delightful Transformation*

30 Shots of God's Word to Keep You Focused on Christ

rhonda rhea

NEW HOPE
PUBLISHERS
Gospel-Centered. Missions-Driven.

BIRMINGHAM, ALABAMA

New Hope® Publishers
P. O. Box 12065
Birmingham, AL 35202-2065
NewHopeDigital.com
New Hope Publishers is a division of WMU®.

Library of Congress Cataloging-in-Publication Data
Rhea, Rhonda.
 Espresso your faith : 30 shots of God's word to keep you focused on Christ / Rhonda Rhea.
  p. cm.
 ISBN 978-1-59669-366-1 (pbk.)
 1. Christian life--Meditations. I. Title.
 BV4501.3.R455 2013
 248.4--dc23

                          2012034902

Cover and Interior Design: Glynese Northam

ISBN-10: 1-59669-366-5
ISBN-13: 978-1-59669-366-1

N134109 • 0213 • 3M1

Dedication

To my children,
Andy, Jordan, Kaley, Allie, and Daniel
Each whose supercharged faith I've been honored to watch
from its birth, through all the new awakenings, now all flourishing,
active and alive. What a privilege and blessing to watch you grow
and minister, allowing the Lord to work in your lives
in such startling, miraculous ways.
You bless me more than I could ever express-o.

Contents

Introduction — Perk Up! 13

Alert, Attentive 17

1. Alert to the Truth — Amazing Glaze 19

2. Alert to the Eternal — In This World, Not Oven It 24

3. Alert to the Prayer Connection — Opening a Can of Terms 29

4. Alert to a Connection with the Church —
   Will the Doughnut Be Unbroken? 34

5. Alert to Clear Thinking — O, They Tell Me of an Unclouded Brain 39

6. Alert to Wisdom — To Every Season, There Is a Thing 44

7. Alert to Serving — Coffee Is Served 49

8. Alert to Sharing Your Faith — This Just Makes Good Scents 55

9. Alert to Worship — O Magnify — And Liquefy 60

10. Alert to Loving in His Name — It Is Well with My Role 66

Watchful, Wide Awake 69

11. Alert to His Coming — What a Way to Go 71

12. Alert to the Enemy — Who's Calling the Shots? 77

13. Alert to Hope — Hope Springs Internal 82

14. Alert to Grace — *Venti, Vidi, Vici* 88

15. Alert to Temptation — Tempted and Tried, Keep Wide the Stride 93

16. Alert to the Needs of Others — What Gives? 98

17. Alert to Forgiveness — What's Your Grind? 103

18. Alert to a Life Change — Something to Write Home About 108

19. Alert to the Devastation of Sin — Faith That Digs In 113

20. Alert to Expecting the Best — Filled Cup, Chin Up 118

Prepared, Primed 119

21. Alert to Judgment — Half and Half and Half   125

22. Alert to Perseverance — Is It Live or Is It Mimeograph?   130

23. Alert to Growing — Only My Barista Knows for Sure   135

24. Alert to Staying Faithful in Hard Times — Fall Up, Not Apart   140

25. Alert to Thankfulness — Thanks a Latte   145

26. Alert to Building Good Character — We Don't Know Beans   150

27. Alert to Strength — *Coffeetizing* to a Stronger Place   155

28. Alert to Keeping the Faith — Steady as She Grows   157

29. Alert to Discipline — Hot and Cold Running Faith   164

30. Alert to God's Ways — Café Before Beauty?   169

Discussion Guide   173

Leader Notes

Guide

A SIMPLE THANK-YOU just doesn't cut it. Überthanks to Richie Rhea, my husband, pastor, counselor, encourager, inspiration, and hero. And to my amazing fam, much love and gratitude for encouragement, support—and a wealth of material: Andy Rhea, Jordan Rhea, Kaley Rhea, Daniel Rhea, and newlyweds Allie Rhea McMullin and Derek McMullin.

Much gratitude to my prayer team for faithfully praying for this book, its readers, and all the other aspects of ministry to boot. There's simply no way to accurately value the time these women have invested on their knees. My humble thanks to Janet Bridgeforth, Tina Byus, Diane Campbell, Mary Clark, Theresa Easterday, Chris Hendrickson, Melinda Massey, and Peanuts Rudolph.

Hugs of gratitude to sweet friend and amazing agent Pamela Harty, and to all those at The Knight Agency who help make it possible for me to do what I do.

A grateful shout-out to Andrea Mullins, Joyce Dinkins, Sherry Hunt, Bruce Watford, Tina Atchenson, Glynese Northam, Hannah Shoop, and all the wonderful folks at New Hope Publishers. I'm challenged and encouraged by your hearts for service and your love for Jesus.

A special nod of thanks to Kaley Rhea (kaleyfaithrhea.com), whose brain is much too much like mine—a little twisted, *mwah ah ah*. Many thanks for time invested as "quip consultant" on this project and as co-author on other projects. The Kaley-chickie helps make them all so much fun.

More thanks to the Advanced Writers and Speakers Association for sharing knowledge, prayers, support, encouragement, and counsel. Love these women!

And many thanks once again to Josh Uecker at New Life 91.9 in Charlotte, North Carolina (newlife919.com), for the continued on-air insanity, and for giving so much material a sort of test run.

Additional thank-yous to my good friends and fellow laborers at *The Pathway*, the Missouri Baptist Convention's official news journal (mbcpathway.com), *The St. Louis MetroVoice* (metrovoice.net), *The Christian Pulse* (thechristianpulse.com), *Inspire Magazine* (inspirestl.com) Living Light News in Edmonton, Alberta, Canada (livinglightnews.org), *Gospel Roads Magazine* (gospelroads.com) and *SBC Life* magazine (sbclife.org). Thank you for your gracious support and for giving me column space for some delicious nonsense—and for kindly supporting me in resharing some of that nonsense in this book.

Over and above, ever and always, my biggest gratitude goes to my Lord and Savior Jesus Christ—who constantly proves through my life that He truly can use absolutely anyone. How honored and blessed I am to be called His child and to be able to do what I do. I have the best job in the world. Thanks, praise, glory, and honor to Jesus!

I think my love language is cappuccino.

INTRO

Perk Up!

THE ANSWER IS coffee. I won't know the question until I've had another cup.

Who would've thought coffee would become such a pronounced connector of generations? Old men, teen girls, corporate execs—blue collar, white collar, rainbow collars—all loving their coffee! Suddenly our fave beverage has become all the more hip, happening, and trendy.

Having trouble looking cool? The right cup and you've got it. Instant cool. Just add coffee.

I had a keen revelation recently: 16 waking hours in a day, 16 cups in two pots of coffee. Coincidence? I think not. I'm not convinced the sun rises in full until there's coffee in my cup.

In my faith-life, however, I want to be more than merely conscious. I want to be revved! Jazzed! Energized! Ready!

"Be alert!" When it's the heavenly Father's tap on the shoulder, we need to be ready to perk up and speedily attend to whatever He's calling us to. The call to alertness runs all through God's Word. First Corinthians 16:13 (AMP) holds an amazing alertness charge: "Be alert and on your guard; stand firm in your faith (your conviction respecting man's relationship to God and divine things, keeping the trust and holy fervor born of faith and a part of it). Act like men and be courageous; grow in strength!"

Not long ago, I was pondering the Lord's charge to be actively alert to so many important aspects of life. If He has given distinctive attention to highlighting special matters we need to stay alert to, it struck me how very vital those things must be if we want to grow closer to Him, to succeed in the walk of faith—to "grow in strength." As I searched terms such as *alert* and *wake up*, I got revved all the more about those faith-life essentials. It was a little like a big gulp of biblical caffeine! Only with no side effects.

Want a stronger faith? Learning to "live alert" can revolutionize our walk with Christ. We can wake up to new ways to honor the Lord as key points from God's Word act as holy espresso. First Peter 5:8 (*The Message*) tells us to "stay alert" and to "keep a firm grip on the faith." As we consume His instructions, we warm up more and more to staying alert and to becoming ever stronger in how we walk out our faith. All the while, He gloriously energizes our lives. Perkier, healthier, stronger—one cup at a time!

Taking on 30 biblical charges to stay alert is a blessed way to strengthen us and to lead us to a place of spiritual maturity. Ready to dive into those biblical charges? We can drink them in. We can let them change us. That place of spiritual maturity is a place where it doesn't matter what kind of hot water we're in, we still stay strong. We never, never, never give up! There is an extraordinary opportunity for delightful faith-growth at every biblical call to attention. Let's not miss a one.

Take a look at this stay-awake charge in 1 Thessalonians 5:5–11 (NLT):

For you are all children of the light and of the day; we don't belong to darkness and night. So be on your guard, not asleep like the others. Stay alert and be clearheaded. Night is the time when people sleep and drinkers get drunk. But let us who live in the light be clearheaded, protected by the armor of faith and love, and wearing as our helmet the confidence of our salvation. For God chose to save us through our Lord Jesus Christ, not to pour out his anger on us. Christ died for us so that, whether we are dead or alive when he returns, we can live with him forever. So encourage each other and build each other up, just as you are already doing.

Perking up already!

Heavenly Father, You know each of us inside out and upside down. You know every single area where our faith needs to grow. You know everything—every desire, every secret, every corner of every heart. You know every success and every heartbreaking disappointment. You know all the places of weakness, and You know exactly how to strengthen those weaknesses and how to build them into testimonies of victory, by your grace, strength, mercy, love, and power. I ask for each reader, Father, that you would do those miraculous works of powerful, unexplainable, life-changing faith building. We look to You to lead us into real life and to build those glorious testimonies, all by Your power and for Your glory and praise. In the ever-prevailing name of Jesus, amen.

Alert,
Attentive

Anytime my feet are a little puffy, I just assume
I'm retaining coffee.

Alert to the Truth
— Amazing Glaze

"Don't be gullible in regard to smooth-talking evil. Stay alert like this" (ROMANS 16:19 *THE MESSAGE*).

WOULDN'T IT BE nice if people came with dashboard lights? First thing in the morning, my "low coffee level" indicator button would no doubt light up. By noon another light would probably flash telling me I'm about a quart low.

My best definition of coffee: hot consciousness with cream and sugar. And I've noticed there are hardly any mornings when consciousness doesn't come in really handy.

I've also noticed that my poor husband misses his on Sundays. His consciousness, that is. There are several things people don't tell you about being a pastor's wife. I can't believe, for instance, that no one ever told me about PTSS. That's how we refer to it around my house anyway. It's post-traumatic sermon syndrome, and it hits every Sunday soon after my husband finishes preaching the last of our three Sunday morning services. He sort of glazes over. There's no indicator light but the whole family knows it. And I know what you're thinking, but there's simply not enough coffee. Not even espresso has the power to unglaze at that point.

Amazing Glaze, How Sweet the Scene
PTSS sounds a little tragic, so I'm not sure how to say this without seeming like a terrible person, but our family has always enjoyed observing the glaze. We're a little twisted that way. It's just that it's often been one of our

family's most entertaining times of the week. Richie is adorably hilarious when he's about a quart low on consciousness.

After three sermons, I've seen my husband go through the drive-through at McDonald's and try to order our lunch by speaking into the trash can. I've seen him leave his car running in the parking lot of a restaurant. I've heard him misspell his own name. This week? OK, this was a good one. Richie was trying to guess who my son was texting. He told us later that for some reason, he was going to ask him if it was "animal, vegetable, or mineral." That was funny all by itself. But it was even better when he asked, "Is it rock, paper, or gas?"

Wait. Now what is it we're made of?

Rock Solid

I guess it's a good reminder that we need to stay alert and give some extra thought to what we're made of. When trouble hits, do we let our faith crumple like paper? Do we see it evaporate away like gas? Or are we rock solid? A rock solid faith is one that stays firmly anchored to Jesus, trusting in the truth of who He is and in the truth of what He says in His Word.

David wrote,

> Guide me in Your truth and faithfulness and teach me, for You are the God of my salvation; for You [You only and altogether] do I wait expectantly all the day long. All the paths of the Lord are mercy and steadfast love, even truth and faithfulness are they for those who keep His covenant and His testimonies (PSALM 25:5, 10 AMP).

We're guided into His truth as we allow His Word to fill our minds and influence the way we live. There is such blessing in filling our lives with His truth. As we see ourselves awakening all the more to His Word, and as we meditate on it more and more, we understand more about Him. We understand that He not only speaks truth, but that He indeed is truth. We see that He is a heavenly Father who always keeps His promises. We see our relationship with Him becoming sweeter and closer because we understand on a deeper level how utterly and completely we can trust

Him. Worries suddenly seem a little silly. Difficulties look smaller. He chooses to reveal Himself to those who seek Him, who seek His guidance and His truth, those who desire to obey. The paths of those who seek Him are "mercy and steadfast love, even truth and faithfulness."

Powering Up

A life steeped in His truth is one of power. People who are alert to His truth learn to make choices that are guided by His principles. They're much less vulnerable to lies.

Paul talks about divisive, trouble-making people in Romans 16:18. These were people with the goal of glazing over the truth and leading others to believe lies. A different kind of glaze that was anything but sweet. "For such people are not serving our Lord Christ, but their own appetites. By smooth talk and flattery they deceive the minds of naïve people." In verse 19 Paul says, "but I want you to be wise about what is good, and innocent about what is evil."

We stay alert to truth by not being persuaded by evil, by not swallowing lies. And we can only recognize the lie as we immerse ourselves into what is true. God's Word will make us wise about what is good and will help us recognize evil. It's God's Holy Spirit who will give us the strength we need to steer clear of that evil and to stay on track in the truth.

All In

Could I encourage you to invest time and energy into building the truth of God into your life? Go all in. At the very moment you pick up His Word, there are likely a thousand distractions clamoring for your attention. Many of them seem so urgent. But I can guarantee you that not one of them is more urgent than what the Father can offer you in His truth. He offers you a well-grounded, rock-solid faith. And that beats any of those distractions.

And just for the record, whatever the glaze, no doubt a rock-solid faith beats paper and gas too.

STAYING AWAKE IN HIS WORD

How can a young man keep his way pure? By living according to your word. I seek you with all my heart; do not let me stray from your commands. I have hidden your word in my heart that I might not sin against you. Praise be to you, O Lord; teach me your decrees. With my lips I recount all the laws that come from your mouth. I rejoice in following your statutes as one rejoices in great riches. I meditate on your precepts and consider your ways. I delight in your decrees; I will not neglect your word.

— Psalm 119:9–16

The coffee-filled piñata.
It looked like such a good idea on paper.

2

"Set your mind on things above, not on earthly things"
(COLOSSIANS 3:2).

MY MICROWAVE DIED yesterday morning. Don't try to console me because I really don't see how we could possibly survive this. I actually half expected the universe would collapse on itself by dinner. At one point I stood there, staring helplessly at my cold cup of coffee. Then at the broken microwave. Then the coffee. Microwave. Coffee. What was I supposed to do? Candle heat? Rub two sticks together? Try a flint rock? I was convinced that my life might never be the same.

I'm not sure how, but we pulled through until dinner. Through the entire day, though, I felt so very *Little House on the Prairie*. And while I loved the show, I'll just tell you right now, this is not my happy place. At some point I fear I'll likely be forced to use the . . . wait, what's this thing called? . . . oh yeah, the "stove." Let's just say I'm not exactly at home on the range.

Out of My Range

Never mind the investment we made in it, I still think I could get rid of the stove altogether. Then again, someone told me that would be "de-ranged." Besides, sometimes I keep my Tupperware in there. You know—all those dishes I like to use . . . *in my microwave.*

It's one more reminder that this world is not my home. Anyway you cook it, life here is as temporary as the things in it. There are many places where we can find joy in this journey. But our one true and lasting happy place? It's just not here. Can't manufacture it. Can't nuke it. Can't buy it. Can't reach it. Talk about out of range. We only find that place of stable joy on this life journey as we learn to stay alert to things eternal and to let everything temporary remind us again to be in this world, not of it

Alert and Sober Reminder

First Peter 1:13–14 is one of those reminders.

> *Therefore, with minds that are alert and fully sober, set your hope on the grace to be brought to you when Jesus Christ is revealed at his coming. As obedient children, do not conform to the evil desires you had when you lived in ignorance.*

Conforming to that old worldly way is not an option. We're instructed to be alert as we put our hope in the complete and all-encompassing grace of Jesus. That's the kind of alertness that keeps us from getting distracted from what's really important by everything trivial. *The Message* paraphrases a charge in Colossians 3:2 to "look up, and be alert to what is going on around Christ—that's where the action is. See things from his perspective."

The verse right before says, "So if you're serious about living this new resurrection life with Christ, act like it. Pursue the things over which Christ presides. Don't shuffle along, eyes to the ground, absorbed with the things right in front of you" (Colossians 3:1 *The Message*).

Alert to Shiny Distractions

To be in the world and not of it requires an alertness to what we're pursuing and how we're looking at life. It's clear that we are to stay in this world as long as the Lord calls us to. We have a mission to share Christ with those who don't know Him and to love people in His name. Our goal should always be to serve Him wholeheartedly and to accomplish every single thing He has planned for us to do.

Accomplishing that goal involves chasing after Him and after His calling—and not chasing after the world, its philosophies, and all the shiny "things" in it. First Thessalonians 5:6 (AMP) says, "Accordingly then, let us not sleep, as the rest do, but let us keep wide awake (alert, watchful, cautious, and on our guard) and let us be sober (calm, collected, and circumspect)." Alert to whatever He's cooking up!

I think it pleases our Father when we delight in all the "lovelies" of this world. He blesses us with good things to enjoy. Even some of those shiny things. But at the point those things become more important than our mission or at the point they distract us from the calling to be about that mission, they become a stumbling block. Those stumbling blocks are sneaky too. Temporary worldly things can become distracting hindrances without us even realizing we're distracted.

Changing the Half-Baked Way We Think

Paul tells us how to get rid of the distractions in Romans 12:2 (NLT):

> Don't copy the behavior and customs of this world, but let God transform you into a new person by changing the way you think. Then you will learn to know God's will for you, which is good and pleasing and perfect.

Distractions lose their power to distract as we focus on the Lord and allow Him to transform our thinking. It's not even about trying to change our own minds. It's about filling our minds with Jesus and allowing Him to do the changing.

As we keep our eyes on Christ, alert to Him and His calling, He is faithful to bring to our attention those things that could interrupt our relationship with Him and interrupt our service for Him. When our full focus is on Him, the extreme "temporariness" of the things of the world becomes crystal clear.

First Timothy 6:7 reminds us, "For we brought nothing into the world, and we can take nothing out of it." That certainly puts those shiny, temporary things in perspective, doesn't it? I guarantee that you won't see me heaving a new microwave onto a shoulder so I can haul it up to Glory with me. Nope. Totally won't need it. For one thing, I'm guessing the coffee is always hot in heaven. For another, successfully walking in faith is so often simply about understanding with alert assurance that there's nothing here that I'll need there. Being with Jesus for eternity will be the ultra-ultimate, überhappy place.

Incidentally, back on this side of heaven, we're heading for one of my secondary happy places tomorrow. It's one of those Appliances-R-Us type stores. It's that or eat out. Every meal.

 ## STAYING AWAKE IN HIS WORD

Don't love the world's ways. Don't love the world's goods. Love of the world squeezes out love for the Father. Practically everything that goes on in the world — wanting your own way, wanting everything for yourself, wanting to appear important — has nothing to do with the Father. It just isolates you from him. The world and all its wanting, wanting, wanting is on the way out — but whoever does what God wants is set for eternity.

— 1 JOHN 2:15–17 (*THE MESSAGE*)

Coffee bean. Cocoa bean.
Bean=protein. Protein=health.
Therefore, mocha can totally save your life.

Alert to the Prayer Connection
— Opening a Can of Terms

3

"Devote yourselves to prayer, being watchful and thankful"
(COLOSSIANS 4:2).

I WAS COFFEEING up for radio the other morning when it occurred to me I get about twice as many words into every two-minute segment when properly coffee-ed. I also noticed that radio is quite delicious. People have told me that a day will still begin even without coffee. I have yet to test that theory.

Sunrise. Coffee. For me the terms are pretty much interchangeable. My day mostly begins sometime after I open up the bag of coffee. I'm very thankful the cans and bags my coffee comes in are not childproof. I don't see how I could possibly open up the coffee before having my coffee.

Since I Have This Opening

On the opening topic, I read somewhere that when a man can't open a jar, he has to throw it away and never speak of it again. Another guy told me that if he can't open a jar, he comes back with a blunt instrument. What is it with guys looking for any excuse to crank up the chain saw? OK, I do understand a chain saw is not a blunt instrument. Unless, of course, you use it to try to pry open a jar.

I admit I personally have an extremely underdeveloped jar-opening muscle. It's withered away from lack of use. That's because I've been married all these years to a really great jar-opener. When Richie is out of town for any length of time, I'm in a real pickle, jar-wise. Not a pickle jar. A pickle. Jar-wise.

Grand Opening

On the spiritual side of the story, however, I'm all about opening up. I never want to neglect exercising my faith by keeping a prayer connection with the Father open and active. We need to build spiritual muscle or we become withered, wimpy semibelievers who shrivel at the slightest pressure. It's true, if we want to keep our spiritual muscle operating at full capacity, we have to consistently pray, thanking and praising Him, loving Him with our thoughts and words, trusting Him with every need, struggle and hurt, staying confessed up and ever open and transparent before Him.

Allowing *prayer* to become merely a churchy word can happen all too readily. It's easy to let it become more about what we want, or what we want others to think we're doing, or what we say we'll do, or even what we intend to do, than it is about communing with the heavenly Father. How sad that it can become a ritualistic, empty religious duty in our hearts and minds, rather than the enormously high privilege and sweet exchange that it truly is meant to be.

Anytime we find ourselves stuck in a prayer funk, we need to give ourselves a little tap on the shoulder—a reminder of our vital need to open up those lines of communication and to see our intimacy restored. Paul said in Colossians 4:2, "Devote yourselves to prayer."

In Terms of Openness

We need to get extreme in that devotion, and to stay extreme in our desperate desire to faithfully connect with the Father, heart to heart. Romans 12:11–12 says, "Never be lacking in zeal, but keep your spiritual fervor, serving the Lord. Be joyful in hope, patient in affliction, faithful in prayer." We're to serve with zeal. It makes sense that our zeal would be so closely connected to our faithfulness in prayer. Dictionaries describe that zeal as enthusiastic devotion and diligence, tirelessly passionate about a cause, idea, person, or goal. That's the kind of passion we want to take with us every time we enter our prayer closet.

We're told in 1 Peter 4:7 (AMP) to "keep sound minded and self-restrained and alert therefore for the practice of prayer." It's our call to alertness.

O Father, remind us every day of our need to stay alert to prayer. Open our eyes to the urgency of our prayer connection with You. May we love You with our prayer lives, and may we love You with great zeal.

Spiritual No-Doze

Just before Jesus went to the Cross, He went to Gethsemane to pray. He took Peter, James and John with Him and told them, "My soul is swallowed up in sorrow—to the point of death. Remain here and stay awake" (Mark 14:34 HCSB). When Jesus came back from His anguished prayer, His disciples had fallen asleep. "Stay awake and pray so that you won't enter into temptation. The spirit is willing, but the flesh is weak," Jesus told them (verse 38). He went to pray again, and again He came back and found them dozing. Then it happened a third time.

Jesus had given them instruction to stay awake and pray and they simply couldn't keep from dozing off. But the Lord's instructions were about more than physical z's. He wanted them to stay alert to what was happening in spiritual places. And He wants us to stay spiritually alert and prayerful still today.

Pep of Faith

A peppier faith and an alert prayer life is not just about avoiding dozing off physically. It's not about finding the right term or phrasing just the right sentence. It's about our passion for the Lord. We need to stay alert to . . . well, to staying alert. A sluggish or apathetic spirit may squeeze out our passion for Christ now and again, but if we want to please the Lord, serve Him successfully and fruitfully live in His joy, we need to be all about getting right back on track in opening that prayer closet door. That's one thing we can always open on our own. With a grateful and expectant heart. And it's the sure way out of any spiritual pickle.

Of course, now I've gotten myself all hungry for pickles. Guess I'd better call my husband. Somebody's got to open this jar.

STAYING AWAKE IN HIS WORD

Pray at all times (on every occasion, in every season) in the Spirit, with all manner of prayer and entreaty. To that end keep alert and watch with strong purpose and perseverance, interceding in behalf of all the saints (God's consecrated people).

— EPHESIANS 6:18 (AMP)

Sleep? Just a crutch for people who don't drink coffee.

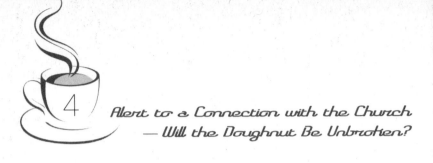

"The human body has many parts, but the many parts make up one whole body. So it is with the body of Christ"

(1 Corinthians 12:12 NLT).

COFFEE AND DOUGHNUTS. They go together like love and marriage. Especially chocolate-filled doughnuts. There's something incredibly beautiful about breakfast with a touch of fudge. Someday I'd like to write a poem and I'd like to start it with the line, "Coffee and doughnuts, sittin' in a tree." I'm not sure where to go from there. I get that far and all I know is that I want to be in that tree.

I confess I've had a few too many doughnuts lately. Sad to say, the bough on that tree would be bending pretty low about now. It's not that I'm not in shape. After all, round is still a shape. But I decided to go on yet another diet recently anyway. I'm embarrassed to tell you I've already fallen off the wagon. Being rounder than I used to be, at least it was a little easier. I could simply *roll* off the wagon.

Circle the Wagons

I'm thinking of putting up a sign that says, "Please keep body inside the wagon at all times, and please stay seated until the wagon comes to a complete and final stop."

You know, if someone would think of bringing fudge along on the wagon ride I would be a lot more motivated to stay on it. OK, I suppose a really good friend would probably give me a nudge to stay on the wagon. Nudge or fudge. Tough call on which is best, friendship-wise.

In our spiritual lives, we all need a little nudge now and then too. It's good to have people in our lives we can count on to nudge us in the right direction, wherever the wagons are heading.

As pioneers were settling the west, when they were threatened by an enemy, circling the wagons was part of their defense strategy. The circle provided a protected cover they could get behind to fire at their attackers.

We need to rally with those on this life's journey in the same way. We have a common enemy. Peter reminds us to "be alert" because our "enemy the devil prowls around like a roaring lion looking for someone to devour" (1 Peter 5:8). Circle the wagons! Our church family is part of our defensive plan against our enemy. The next verse in 1 Peter says, "Resist him, standing firm in the faith, because you know that the family of believers throughout the world is undergoing the same kind of sufferings" (v. 9).

Will the Circle Be Unbroken?

We're in this together. Let's not neglect circling the wagons. "Not forsaking or neglecting to assemble together as believers, as is the habit of some people, but admonishing (warning, urging, and encouraging) one another, and all the more faithfully as you see the day approaching" (Hebrews 10:25 AMP).

I'm so thankful the Lord has placed godly church buds and godly leaders in my path all through my life via the church. People with just the right nudge at the ready. There are pastors and teachers who stay alert to our spiritual supervision, keeping watch the Scripture says. And Hebrews 13:17 instructs us to be responsive to them. "Have confidence in your leaders and submit to their authority, because they keep watch over you as those who must give an account. Do this so that their work will be a joy, not a burden, for that would be of no benefit to you."

More Than Just a Circle

As believers, we are part of each other in the body of Christ. Paul tells us in 1 Corinthians 12:27: "Now you are the body of Christ, and each one of you is a part of it." The body of Christ is so much more than just a defense against a common enemy. It's an amazing entity. Not an organization. An *organism*. Living. Each part vital. When we unite, connected in our common calling, and use the individual gifts God has given us as we work together to accomplish that calling, the enemy loses. The body functions, with Christ as its head, and God the Father is glorified.

Not one of us should ever decide that the body is fine without each person doing its part. When we fail to link in and do our share, it's like robbing the body of a significant part. Who wants to leave the body of Christ without a leg or an arm?

Whether your part in the body of Christ is one that garners a lot of attention or one that often goes unnoticed, never underestimate your importance to the body's effective functioning. Or anyone else's either. Paul tells us in 1 Corinthians 12:20–22,

> *As it is, there are many parts, but one body. The eye cannot say to the hand, 'I don't need you!' And the head cannot say to the feet, 'I don't need you!' On the contrary, those parts of the body that seem to be weaker are indispensable.*

Loving each other and staying attached to the body is important to the Lord. You were plugged into all believers, Christ's church, when you accepted Him as your Savior. It's important, too, that you plug in to a body of believers in a local church. We need each other and we're more fruitful when we work together. It's not always easy. But it's vital. And it's our calling. In Ephesians 4:1–3 (HCSB), Paul urges us to walk worthy of the "calling" we've received, "with all humility and gentleness, with patience, accepting one another in love, diligently keeping the unity of the Spirit with the peace that binds us."

"Diligently," Paul said. That seems like one of those highly caffeinated words to me.

O Lord, help us to be intentional about carefully, enthusiastically, industriously, diligently keeping the unity of Your Spirit with the peace that binds us.

Wagonistas Learn to Wear the Wagon Well

I should go ahead and confess here that I will likely not be nearly as diligent as I should about rolling on and off that diet wagon. The *circle* in circling the wagons still makes me think of a doughnut.

I'm considering keeping the doughnuts and the extra 20 pounds and just getting myself a bigger wagon. One with really good shocks.

 STAYING AWAKE IN HIS WORD

Let's see how inventive we can be in encouraging love and helping out, not avoiding worshiping together as some do but spurring each other on, especially as we see the big Day approaching. Be responsive to your pastoral leaders. Listen to their counsel. They are alert to the condition of your lives and work under the strict supervision of God. Contribute to the joy of their leadership, not its drudgery. Why would you want to make things harder for them?

— HEBREWS 10: 24–25; 13:17 (*THE MESSAGE*)

One cup of coffee, one eye opens. Two cups, two eyes open. Three cups . . . Wait. I'm going to need more eyes.

Alert to Clear Thinking
— O, They Tell Me of an Unclouded Brain

SOME MORNINGS I wake up thinking all my brain cells might've gotten a little moldy during the night. I keep thinking enough coffee will surely flush everything furry from the gray matter. Of course, we're talking about a lot of coffee here. Sometimes it would be nice if I could declog my brain like I clean out my vacuum cleaner.

I had a little wrestling match with the vacuum recently. It was doing that wimpy-clean thing—you know, where you have to get down on your hands and knees and hand-feed it every little fuzz ball? If I'm going to do that, I might as well not have a vacuum cleaner. I could just pick up every little piece of fuzz and throw it all in the trash myself, couldn't I? Cut out the middle man.

A vacuum that's lost all its *suck-ocity* is not worth much. So I got down on the floor, got the thing in a headlock, and looked inside to find out what the problem might be. Oh, I found a problem alright. Several.

What's the Matter with This Gray Matter?
First of all, why are the contents of a vacuum cleaner always gray? It doesn't matter what color your carpet is. Doesn't matter what color dirt you've tracked in. The vacuum dirt is always gray. What is that? Every once in a while I kind of wonder if I lost my mind, then vacuumed it up. Gross.

Amongst all the disgusting gray matter, I found a problematic little lump of sock. Then there was that piece of string. While I call it a string, I think it might better be described as a length of yarn that could've been an entire sweater in another life. There was a hunk of the bathroom rug the size of a Chihuahua. An entire section of rug missing and I hadn't even noticed? Weird.

I was also surprised to find what I thought was a loofa. But then I realized it was just a whole bunch of those little plastic fishing-line-like connectors that attach price tags to things. Who knew they could find each other inside the dark recesses of the vacuum cleaner and form their own little solar system? No wonder the machine didn't want to work! How did all that stuff even get in there?

Declogging Our Minds

At least it gave me a little reminder. When we let our minds suck up the wrong things, we can't expect them to work the way they're supposed to either. We need to stay alert to emptying out the dirt clods and alert to filling our minds with the kinds of thoughts that truly feed our spirits and grow our faith.

Negative, evil thoughts will find each other in the dark recesses of our minds. And they multiply. The next thing you know, you find yourself with a solar-system-sized problem in your thought life.

There's so much garbage available to us. On the Internet, TV, movies, magazines—it's accessible at every turn of the head. If we let our minds continually suck up trashy junk, we shouldn't be surprised when we have a hard time staying alert to walking out our faith-life well.

Steering Clear of Fluff-headedness

It's not just a matter of emptying our minds. No one wants to stay empty-headed. We don't want our minds filled with mere fluff either. It's about filling our minds well. Paul tells us in Philippians 4:8–9 what kind of things we're supposed to continually feed our minds:

Finally, brothers and sisters, whatever is true, whatever is noble, whatever is right, whatever is pure, whatever is lovely, whatever is admirable—if anything is excellent or praiseworthy—think about such things. Whatever you have learned or received or heard from me, or seen in me—put it into practice. And the God of peace will be with you.

There's a lot less wrestling with our minds when we remember to fill them with the right things. Less wrestling, more peace. As a matter of fact, that passage doesn't simply say that we'll experience great peace, it tells us that the God of peace Himself will be "with" us. It's vital to our faith-life that we remember that His presence makes all the difference.

Alert to a Jesus-focus

Sometimes negative thoughts are sneaky. They're not blatantly dark. But they're deceptively full of self. And that sucks us right back into those dark places. I have to ask myself often which interests me more. Is my life about loving Jesus? Or are my thoughts more focused on what He can do for me? Am I more concerned with the blessings He can give me right now than I am focused on knowing Him more and loving Him better?

When Jesus walked this planet, He often encountered people who couldn't quite get their focus off what He could do for them. The crowds were always after Him—mostly wanting a quick fix for whatever ailed them.

It's not that their needs weren't legitimate—and it's not that we're not instructed to ask the Lord to meet our needs. We are to humbly come to Jesus with our every need. We're to come to Him not demanding He meet our needs and fix our problems and make our lives easy and lined with all the nicest fluff, but asking for our needs to be met and then fully relying on Him to determine what our needs are. It's really about allowing Him to clear out the clogging fluff and let us fully understand that every real need is already met in Christ.

Could I encourage you not to use your prayer time to try to selfishly get what you want? Use it to get to know your Savior better—pursuing a sweet intimacy with Him. Our desire to have Him grant our requests in just the way we want should never drown out our willingness to follow Him—wherever He may lead, whatever His will may be. That's clearly the clearheaded path.

And personally, I think it's also clear I need to clean out my vacuum a little more often. When I was unclogging it, even though we've never had one, I'm pretty sure I found a gerbil.

STAYING AWAKE IN HIS WORD

Jesus answered, "Very truly I tell you, you are looking for me, not because you saw the signs I performed but because you ate the loaves and had your fill. Do not work for food that spoils, but for food that endures to eternal life, which the Son of Man will give you. For on him God the Father has placed his seal of approval."

Then they asked him, "What must we do to do the works God requires?"

Jesus answered, "The work of God is this: to believe in the one he has sent."

So they asked him, "What sign then will you give that we may see it and believe you? What will you do? Our ancestors ate the manna in the wilderness; as it is written: 'He gave them bread from heaven to eat.'"

Jesus said to them, "Very truly I tell you, it is not Moses who has given you the bread from heaven, but it is my Father who gives you the true bread from heaven. For the bread of God is the bread that comes down from heaven and gives life to the world.'

"Sir," they said, "always give us this bread."

Then Jesus declared, "I am the bread of life. Whoever comes to me will never go hungry, and whoever believes in me will never be thirsty. But as I told you, you have seen me and still you do not believe. All those the Father gives me will come to me, and whoever comes to me I will never drive away."

— JOHN 6:26–37

Coffee + computer = some words in a book.

"Live wisely . . . awake and ready for me each morning,
alert and responsive as I start my day's work"
(PROVERBS 8:32, 34 *THE MESSAGE*).

I HEARD SOMEONE talking about making coffee from green beans the other day. I hope they were referring to coffee beans harvested early and not the vegetable. Because then next would probably come lima bean coffee or something like that and I can't think of any season when that would be wise.

People can be funny about seasons. I know a gal who only drinks coffee in the winter. That's just not right. Is there some sort of seasonal coffee disorder? I want to tell her—with entirely too much enthusiasm—it's a cup of coffee. Not a wool scarf. This is not a "white shoes after Labor Day" kind of situation. To every drink there is a season. And coffee is all of them.

Season-in-a-Box

Why is it we tend to put some things in a seasonal box where they don't belong, and not include others that really do? For instance, there comes a moment in the spring I feel the need to announce to my girlfriends: "We're officially into the warm season. Time to get rid of the leg fur." Well, actually, I'm only tempted to announce it to those of my friends I happen to know to be seasonal shavers. When your legs look more like the wool scarf than the wool scarf does, it's time to rethink your season schedule anyway.

The fitness routine is another one of those things we make seasonal when it's not supposed to be. It's usually inspired by the impending doom of the swimsuit time of year. "Exercise" and "swimsuit season" go together like kidney stones and strong painkillers.

I know you're thinking I'm not qualified to give insights into anything fitness-related. And that's true. But while I might not get a whole lot of exercise, I'll have you know I flipped my hair with a whole lot of exuberance just this morning. I may be sore tomorrow.

It's interesting that the body itself has seasons too. For instance, I've noticed it's now OK for me to wear skin-tight outfits. These days my skin actually fits more like scrubs. If skin-tight means scrub-tight, we're OK. Except for the sadness of a scrub-fitting body. I'm not sure how much of it has to do with my age and how much of it is more about my fitness disciplines. Either way, it's why I'm forced to ever fear the season of sleeveless tops. I guess every season has its thing.

Life and Favor, Life with Flavor

Wisdom? It's different. It always fits. There's no "out season" for real wisdom. We're not talking about the ill-fitting worldly wisdom that's not really wisdom at all but a true understanding of life and all its happenings from God's view. True wisdom is applying and living according to that understanding.

Proverbs 3:21 tells us we should never let wisdom and understanding out of our sight. The next verse says "they will be life for you, an ornament to grace your neck" (Proverbs 3:22). Wool scarf? No, better. Life! And life well-decorated. A few chapters later we read that those who find wisdom "find life and receive favor from the Lord" (Proverbs 8:35). It's life at its most favor-filled and flavor-filled. Delish!

Where's the How-To Manual for Decision Making?

Every day holds a new slate of decisions. How many creams in my coffee? Should I go to college? Can I wear that scarf this late in the season? Should I invest in that friendship? Can I afford that gym membership? Should

I marry that person? Which career should I choose? How should I invest my time today? My money? The choices can be absolutely overwhelming.

Not to worry, though. Your heavenly Father cares about your decisions, and He will be faithful to give you wisdom. Some of your answers are spelled out in black and white within the pages of His Word. Get to know Him through Scripture and many of those choices become crystal clear. We need to ask ourselves often if there are biblical commands and principles we're ignoring in making one decision or another. At every yes answer, we need to be prepared for a quick and complete turnaround.

Earthly "wisdom" will tell you that you need to go with your gut. It says ask yourself how you "feel" about your choice—because, again, earthly wisdom is not wisdom at all. Feelings and emotions are up, down, and all over the place. Boy, are they seasonal. You can't trust them.

Genuine wisdom is trusting in the Father, trusting in His Word, and trusting in His Holy Spirit who lives within you, guiding you in wisdom. It's that wisdom that will lead you down a healthier path. Trust in God, not in your own thoughts, feelings, and emotions. Making a decision because it "feels right" leads countless people into some incredibly dumb moves—often with devastating consequences.

A Word to the Wise — and Those Who Wannabe

If you're wrestling with a decision, it never hurts to check in with friends. Believers who you know to be ardent students of the Word can offer wise counsel. Proverbs 13:20 (HCSB) says, "The one who walks with the wise will become wise."

Ultimately though, the decision is yours to make. You are personally responsible for each choice and for making sure those choices honor God. Living in His wisdom, letting it become a natural part of how we walk out our faith, takes us to a safer place in life. Take a closer look at that Proverbs 3:21–26 passage:

My son, do not let wisdom and understanding out of your sight, preserve sound judgment and discretion; they will be life for you, an ornament to grace your neck. Then you will go on your way in safety, and your foot will not stumble. When you lie down, you will not be afraid; when you lie down, your sleep will be sweet. Have no fear of sudden disaster or of the ruin that overtakes the wicked, for the LORD will be at your side and will keep your foot from being snared.

There is protection in living in His wisdom.

Always the Season for Seeking

Struggling with a decision? Seek wisdom through the counsel of God's Word. His Word ever stands as the user's guide for wisdom. Seek wisdom through the counsel of mature, godly Christians. And never neglect the discipline of seeking wisdom through the counsel of the Father Himself. Seek Him in prayer. James 1:5 (ESV) says, "If any of you lacks wisdom, let him ask God, who gives generously to all without reproach, and it will be given him." There's wisdom right there for the asking. And the psalmist said, "I will bless the LORD who has given me counsel; my heart also instructs me in the night seasons," (Psalm 16:7 NKJV).

You can trust your heart in those night seasons when your heart is filled with His Holy Spirit, completely surrendered to Him.

For the record, I've heard the decision on whether or not we can wear white shoes in the "night seasons" is still up in the air.

STAYING AWAKE IN HIS WORD

For you were once darkness, but now you are light in the Lord. Live as children of light (for the fruit of the light consists in all goodness, righteousness and truth) and find out what pleases the Lord. Have nothing to do with the fruitless deeds of darkness, but rather expose them. It is shameful even to mention what the disobedient do in secret. But everything exposed by the light becomes visible — and everything that is illuminated becomes a light. This is why it is said: "Wake up, sleeper, rise from the dead, and Christ will shine on you." Be very careful, then, how you live — not as unwise but as wise.

— EPHESIANS 5:8–15

If I'm only as strong as the coffee I drink, I'm still good.

Alert to Serving
— Coffee Is Served

"Work with enthusiasm, as though you were
working for the Lord rather than for people"
(EPHESIANS 6:7 NLT).

SOME PEOPLE SAY they *love* coffee. But I've noticed most of them don't seem to be willing to commit.

Personally, I consider myself a high-functioning coffee addict. I don't think anyone truly knows if coffee-holism is treatable. No one has ever been willing to be treated. Still, I think my willingness to be committed is evident. Evidence someone could likely use in a hearing someday to determine if I should be committed in an entirely different sense of the word, but as long as the coffee is strong there, I'll be fine.

For me, coffee isn't quite strong enough until it holds the spoon up by itself. I like it when it's somewhere close to chewy. Coffee you can sink your teeth into.

Commit or Be Committed?

I've heard you can tell a lot about people by the way they take their coffee. Me? I'm all in. Full strength with everything added. A lot of everything. When I order coffee at a restaurant and the waitress asks if I would like cream, I usually tell her yes and that she should bring enough for my four or five friends that I'm not expecting to show up. So if it's true that you can tell a lot about people by their coffee, one of the things mine says about me is that it's unlikely I'll ever have to worry about osteoporosis.

When it comes time to add the sweeteners (yes, plural), I ask my friends, real and imaginary, to look away so I'm sure no one will see how many packet tops I'm tearing off. I confess, I drink it crazy-sweet. Coffee with dessert? How about coffee *for* dessert! Keep giving me sweetener packets and I'll keep enthusiastically pouring them in. While I think of it as supplementing my coffee, others might think of it more as a new way to make syrup. When it's pour-it-over-waffles insanely sweet, it's perfect. That's why I ask everyone to look away. I figure there's no sense piling on any more evidence for that hearing. I may be coffee crazy, but I figure I should at least get points for being enthusiastic about it.

Keep Pouring It In

For our faith to become strong and to stay strong, we need to keep on pouring the right things into our lives with the same kind of enthusiasm.

> *Supplement your faith with a generous provision of moral excellence, and moral excellence with knowledge, and knowledge with self-control, and self-control with patient endurance, and patient endurance with godliness, and godliness with brotherly affection, and brotherly affection with love for everyone. The more you grow like this, the more productive and useful you will be in your knowledge of our Lord Jesus Christ* (2 PETER 1:5–8 NLT).

We're charged here to stay alert to supplementing our lives with everything sweet.

Did you notice how it wraps up with brotherly affection and love for everyone? And did you also notice that all these things work together to make us more productive and help provide a life of usefulness? Loving and serving is at the heart of our faith. Paul said

> *those of us who are strong and able in the faith need to step in and lend a hand to those who falter, and not just do what is most convenient for us. Strength is for service, not status. Each one of us needs to look after*

the good of the people around us, asking ourselves, "How can I help?"
(ROMANS 15:1–2 *THE MESSAGE*).

Satisfied in Service

First Peter 4:10 (ESV) says, "As each has received a gift, use it to serve one another, as good stewards of God's varied grace." The God who knit us together has called each of us to serve—even planned out what He has for each of us to do. We're told in Ephesians 2:10 (NCV), "God has made us what we are. In Christ Jesus, God made us to do good works, which God planned in advance for us to live our lives doing." He planned those works with you in mind. He knit you together to fit your job. And it makes sense that in doing what we were created to do, we find satisfaction and joy in this walk of faith like in nothing else.

David had a heart for service. For the most part, he kept his heart surrendered to God—whatever service the Lord had for him. He served faithfully whether he was sitting in a field with a bunch of sheep or on a throne ruling a kingdom.

Was it easy service? I don't think so. He battled a lion and a bear. He battled a giant. He battled armies and a reigning king who wanted him dead. He battled all kinds of difficulties, big and small. He even had to battle his own flesh. Yet he did it all with great fervor. Sometimes with great success. Sometimes in heartbreaking defeat. But reading the psalms he wrote we see his intense passion. When he was rightly serving the Lord, he poured himself in. All in! Though the persecution, troubles, and his own failures sometimes got him down, David knew real satisfaction as he placed himself fully in the Lord's service. He said in Psalm 109:28 (CEV), "You . . . will make me glad to be your servant."

Supplemental Servants

I've seen many people through the years who initially thought they were too busy for service. Or who thought they were unqualified for service. I've enjoyed those times I could simply watch as God added them to the ranks of the faithful. I've seen Him transform their unwillingness, resistance, doubt, and insecurity into fervor, victory, boldness, and, ultimately, fruit. The catalyst for every transformation was a passionate surrender to serve Him.

Where are you in your service? Are you sweet and strong—like my idea of a good cup of coffee? Or are you one of those unwilling or insecure followers? Surrender to His plan for you. He will give you everything you need at that place of surrender.

The more we get to know our heavenly Father and the more we understand His call to service, the more we understand that He never calls us to do anything He doesn't equip us to do. He "fills our cup," so to speak, with everything we need.

Stop and think for a minute about all the ways God has supplemented your life. Think about how He has put you together. Part of learning to walk in faith is becoming alert to exactly how He has wired you. Your loving Father would never stuff gifts and talents into your life willy-nilly. With great care and thought—and with mind-boggling purpose—He has placed into your cup exactly what you need for what He calls you to do. It's sad to think about all the times we've shifted our brains and our spirits into neutral and ignored the gifts He's given us.

Your gift for music? It's from Him. Your ability to organize? Your uncanny knack for showing mercy to others? From Him! How are you using those for His honor? Your word skills? Your math brain? He wired those. Are you creating words or crunching numbers for His glory? Peter said, "If anyone serves, they should do so with the strength God provides" (1 Peter 4:11). There is an excitement and fulfillment—maybe even the adventure you're longing for—as you recognize the amazing ways He has supplied your life to love Him. What could be sweeter than fulfilling your true purpose and making a real difference in this life?

Coming On Strong

Are you quick to love Him, but slow to serve Him? Then I don't know how to tell you this, but you're not all that quick to love Him. Real love for the Lord shows up in selfless service. Not with eye-rolling, heavy-sighing, and an attitude that says, "If no one else will do it then, fine, I guess I'll have to." Attitude counts. Not reluctance, but alert enthusiasm. "Alert servants of the Master" as *The Message* phrases Romans 12:11. All in!

So let's do it. Let's make it our goal to stay strong in our service. Weak and wimpy? No way! Pour yourself into the kind of service you can sink your teeth into.

 STAYING AWAKE IN HIS WORD

In light of all this, here's what I want you to do. While I'm locked up here, a prisoner for the Master, I want you to get out there and walk — better yet, run! — on the road God called you to travel. I don't want any of you sitting around on your hands. I don't want anyone strolling off, down some path that goes nowhere. And mark that you do this with humility and discipline — not in fits and starts, but steadily, pouring yourselves out for each other in acts of love, alert at noticing differences and quick at mending fences.

— EPHESIANS 4:1–3 (*THE MESSAGE*)

Drinking really strong Romanian coffee this
morning—and so loving it.
Except that I can't seem to blink.

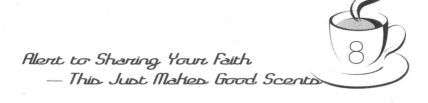

Alert to Sharing Your Faith
— This Just Makes Good Scents

8

> "You were chosen to tell about the wonderful acts of God, who called
> you out of darkness into his wonderful light"
> (1 PETER 2:9 NCV).

MY FAVORITE PLACES to write are coffee shops. There's something about the aroma of so many good coffees that seems to cause more of my neurons to start firing. Somebody should make a scratch-n-sniff version I can take home. But since I haven't found one, when there's a deadline looming, I head to my fave café spot until I'm finished. I think I almost won the employee of the month award there once.

Last time I walked into "my" café just for a fun lunch, I took a long sniff and said, "Mmm, smells like a book deadline in here." Another writer friend fired right back, "Hmm, smells like procrastination to me." *Potato/Po-tah-to.*

I'll Have the Potato/Po-tah-to Soup to Go, Please
They have a great potato soup on the lunch menu at my coffee café. It's not often I have any left over, but I did a few months ago. I packaged it up to take home and got it as far as my car, but then I forgot it. My son borrowed my car for a week or so and the soup ended up shoved way under the seat in the back.

By the time I got back in my car, it made my eyes water. It didn't help that on top of the potato soup stench, Daniel had left several socks in a kind of compost pile. The whole car smelled like the monkey cages at the zoo. This was scratching and sniffing of a whole different order. Some smells are hard to ignore. Even with the windows down. Even with the windows down for several weeks in a row.

Sometimes a to-go order loses something in translation. Or transportation.

The Believer on the Go

In Hebrews 11, the "Hall of Faith," we read that God gave Abraham a to-go order of a different kind. What did Abraham do? He took off! Never mind the where. He packed up his faith and hit the road. "By faith Abraham, when called to go to a place he would later receive as his inheritance, obeyed and went, even though he did not know where he was going" (Hebrews 11:8). What a great example of faith and obedience—going!

We've been given a to-go order too. In John 20:21 the resurrected Jesus said to His followers, "As the Father has sent me, I am sending you." And He made no bones about it in Matthew 28:19–20.

> *Therefore go and make disciples of all nations, baptizing them in the name of the Father and of the Son and of the Holy Spirit, and teaching them to obey everything I have commanded you. And surely I am with you always, to the very end of the age.*

He commands us to go! What a privilege to be sent on such a worthy mission by the Savior Himself.

As we go, we're His billboards. And we're spreading the sweet perfume of Christ at the same time. And this is so much better than anything scratch-n-sniff. "But thanks be to God, who always puts us on display in Christ and through us spreads the aroma of the knowledge of Him in every place" (2 Corinthians 2:14 HCSB). The aroma of Christ! Others are influenced—changed, even, by Christ—when we wear His perfume. We're sent. And we're His scent.

Do Tell, Do Smell

It's not always an easy mission. *The Message* phrases Matthew 10:16 this way: "Stay alert. This is hazardous work I'm assigning you." Hazardous?

Yes. But we're not alone on the mission. As a matter of fact, we don't even have to come up with the right words. A few verses later in that passage we read, "Do not worry about what to say or how to say it. At that time you will be given what to say, for it will not be you speaking, but the Spirit of your Father speaking through you" (Matthew 10:19–20 NIV).

The message for the world has the distinct smell of mercy all over it. What a thrill it is to share it. It's a stunning message of God's love and His sweet embrace. Ephesians 2:4–5 says, "because of his great love for us, God, who is rich in mercy, made us alive with Christ." *The Message* phrases it this way: "immense in mercy and with an incredible love, he embraced us."

God's merciful salvation plan for us is all about His coming near. It's His tender hug. Jesus suffered an excruciating and humiliating death on a cross—a criminal's death. Our perfect, sinless Savior hung on a cross with the crushing weight of our sin placed upon Him, all so we could have a sweet, loving relationship with our holy God.

Staying *Scents-i-tive*

Then God came up with the plan to get the word out about the salvation that's available through that sacrificial death. He could've sent smoke signals. He could've put it on YouTube or done an intense eblast. He could've done it with skywriting. He could've written it in the stars or broadcast it over every satellite. Instead, He chose to bless us by commissioning the job to us. He honored us by allowing us to participate in the sharing plan. And in the light of all He's done to provide our salvation, is it too much to ask that we share it? And considering what's at stake for those with whom we share, how could we even consider keeping quiet?

When a person understands Christ's sacrificial death, genuinely comes to faith, in surrender of every part of life, that life is no longer wrapped up in all the temporary things it used to be. Life takes on new meaning. It's never the same.

If He has made that change in your life, living a Christ-filled, God-changed life before others testifies in and of itself. A changed life is a powerful message. There's a quote that's often attributed to

Francis of Assisi, but no one knows for sure he's the one who said it. Though it's made it around the world in different forms, it rings so very true: "Preach the gospel at all times. If necessary, use words."

Though we should never neglect the *telling*, it's good to remember that our lives are proclaiming what we're all about, even when we're not saying much. We need to make sure the heart message of our lives shines clearly through. And we need to stay *scents-i-tive*, as it were, to the desperate heart-need of a lost and dying world.

Shine It Through, Pray It Through
O Lord, may our lives be permeated with the aroma of Your Son, Jesus, so that those who don't know You will be drawn away from the stench of death to the glorious sweetness of Your love, Your grace, Your mercy!

Isaiah 52:7 (HCSB) tells us it's beautiful when we diffuse the aroma of Christ. "How beautiful on the mountains are the feet of the herald, who proclaims peace, who brings news of good things, who proclaims salvation, who says to Zion, 'Your God reigns!'"

The proclaimers of salvation get to live with beautiful feet. I'm confident it's a no-sock-compost zone.

 STAYING AWAKE IN HIS WORD

I am grateful that God always makes it possible for Christ to lead us to victory. God also helps us spread the knowledge about Christ everywhere, and this knowledge is like the smell of perfume. In fact, God thinks of us as a perfume that brings Christ to everyone. For people who are being saved, this perfume has a sweet smell and leads them to a better life. But for people who are lost, it has a bad smell and leads them to a horrible death.

— 2 Corinthians 2:14–16 (CEV)

*I heard a rumor that coffee cures a
wide range of diseases.
It may not be true, but I just don't see how
I could possibly take that chance.*

9

Alert to Worship
— O Magnify — and Liquefy

"Keep your eyes open for GOD, watch for his works;
be alert for signs of his presence"
(PSALM 105:4 *THE MESSAGE*).

PEOPLE SAY THAT to survive a volatile stock market you should have plenty of liquidity. That's why I'm thinking about investing in water. A few scoops of my favorite grind, a little percolating, and I can contemplate my investment with a cup of coffee!

When you're investing in water stocks, I wonder if you get to decide whether to buy the hydrogen and oxygen together or separately. I don't know; chemistry was never my thing. Knowing me I'd mix up my formulas. A couple of extra dashes of oxygen and instead of H_2O I could end up with something like H_2O_2. That might be a better investment stock-wise, but it falls way short when you're thirsty . . . what with it being hydrogen peroxide and all. Although, bonus. Instead of investing or drinking I could just forget the whole thing and go color my hair.

My Hair Runneth Over
Sometimes I can almost convince myself this is my real hair color. Then again, it's probably just a pigment of my imagination.

I had to laugh one time when I was whining about having to get my hair colored so often and Richie suggested I take some time off from coloring. Husbands. They're so cute. I told him I wasn't ready for that kind of time off. A total gray-cation? No thanks. I'd dye first.

Hair color is one thing, but it's a pretty sure bet nobody wants me messing with chemical elements or any of their atomic structures. There's a rather frightening thought. I do, however, love thinking of Jesus as our "Living H$_2$O." Makes me thirsty just thinking about it.

Color Me Thirsty

Our ardent thirst for the Lord leads us to a place of worship. Worship is our right response every time we contemplate our glorious God and every time we seek Him. When God told Moses to tell Pharaoh, "This is what the LORD says: Let my people go, so they can worship me" (Exodus 8:1), God set in place the plan to free His people. But He didn't simply free them from slavery. He freed them so they could worship Him.

Our salvation came at great cost. God freed us from the slavery of sin so we could worship Him. Not merely freedom *from* something. But freedom *to do* something. Worship. He wants an intimate relationship with each of us in which we recognize Him as the great God of the universe He is. We were built for worshiping Him. And as we do what we were built to do, we find ourselves in the sweetest of sweet spots.

As we thirst for Him, He does satisfy. Jesus said to the woman at the well, "If you knew the gift of God, and who is saying to you, 'Give Me a drink,' you would ask Him, and He would give you living water'" (John 4:10 HCSB).

The more we thirst for Him and seek Him in worship, the more we see the Lord tweak all the other thirsts. Frustrations and challenges, fears and angers, heartaches and failures—they fall into perspective at our altar of worship.

H2Whoa!

In 2 Chronicles 20, King Jehoshaphat was surrounded by a huge army of his enemies. Jehoshaphat responded in a wonderfully thirsty way.

> *Alarmed, Jehoshaphat resolved to inquire of the LORD, and he proclaimed a fast for all Judah. The people of Judah came together to seek help from the LORD; indeed, they came from every town in Judah to seek him* (2 CHRONICLES 20:3–4).

Not only did he seek the Lord, but he rallied the people to worship as well. He sought the Lord's mercy and His help, yes, but in his prayers he also recognized the sovereignty of God, His presence and His goodness. Jehoshaphat confessed in prayer that they had no power to face the vast army but added the faith statement, "but our eyes are on you" (v. 12).

The Lord responded to their worship. He told them they wouldn't even need to fight—that the battle was His. How do you think the people responded to His answer that He would be with them? They worshiped some more! "Jehoshaphat bowed down with his face to the ground, and all the people of Judah and Jerusalem fell down in worship before the LORD" (v. 18).

Then they put together one of the weirdest battle plans ever. Jehoshaphat put the singers on the frontlines. A choir attack? Whoa! They didn't even have squirt guns. It would be especially weird if we didn't know what power there is in praising and worshiping our all-powerful God. The choir's job was to praise God for the splendor of His holiness. And it worked. The enemy armies started killing each other off until not a one was left standing. When the army of Judah arrived, everyone was dead. All that was left to do was collect the spoils.

Going Deeper

There's not a day in this life that each of us doesn't face some battle or another. We're attacked by those fears and worries, stresses and heartbreaks. Sometimes we feel about as overwhelmed as Jehoshaphat and his army. Surrounded.

Let your battle be won in worship. Let praise be your ammo. The battle isn't yours unless you take it back from your Father. Worship the One who will fight for you. Focus your heart and mind in worship of Him who has already won every truly vital victory for you.

Practically speaking, every battle and every thirst calls us to our knees. As you pray, ask God to show Himself to you and to take you straight to His heart in the closest, most adoring worship. Desire it. Thirst for it. Spend time praising and worshipping Him, as well as asking Him to meet your needs. You become like those whose company you keep. Keep company with Jesus. Time with Him daily is absolutely essential to your growth in your walk of faith. As you respond well to the right thirst, you can find yourself plunging into deep waters of worship.

Wade On In

Keep in mind that every moment of worship is about Him. It's easy to get into a wrong pattern of thought, thinking that time spent with Him is really about you. But selfishness is the opposite of worship. Your worship time is not to be about what's in it for you. It's not about seeking a blessing or seeking a cool experience or even seeking an easier life. It's about seeking Him and only Him. Deuteronomy 4:29 (ESV) says that "you will seek the Lord your God and you will find him, if you search after him with all your heart and with all your soul."

Give Him your all in worship. Each moment of surrender is a moment of no regrets. It's a moment of complete fulfillment as you're surrendering to what you were made for and a moment of great fulfillment as you give Him His due. Drink in His astounding goodness and let your worship be the response that gives you a deeper sense of His glorious presence.

So even if the stock market totally dries up, I think I'll forget about all that and simply shoot for staying thirsty for everything Jesus. And I'm not even going to worry about the *H*s or the *O*s.

STAYING AWAKE IN HIS WORD

I appeal to you therefore, brethren, and beg of you in view of all the mercies of God, to make a decisive dedication of your bodies presenting all your members and faculties as a living sacrifice, holy, devoted, consecrated and well pleasing to God, which is your reasonable, rational, intelligent service and spiritual worship. Do not be conformed to this world, this age, fashioned after and adapted to its external, superficial customs, but be transformed, changed by the entire renewal of your mind by its new ideals and its new attitude, so that you may prove for yourselves what is the good and acceptable and perfect will of God, even the thing which is good and acceptable and perfect in His sight for you.

— ROMANS 12:1–2 (AMP)

Breakfast is the most important meal of the day. I'm convinced whatever study revealed this fact was based on coffee alone.

Alert to Loving in His Name
— It Is Well with My Role

> "Pouring yourselves out for each other in acts of love,
> alert at noticing differences and quick at mending fences"
> (EPHESIANS 4:3 *THE MESSAGE*).

I HAD TO battle a stupid flu bug a few weeks ago. It's that bug that seemed to circle the planet a couple of times. I may have gotten it on both trips. I was so not well—coming and going. Our entire household had it the first time through. I felt like I was living in a petri dish. I don't even want to know what kind of culture that was.

Maybe it wouldn't have been so bad if I could've remembered if I was supposed to starve a cold or feed a fever. Or feed the cold maybe, and let the fever go hungry? I finally decided to forget the whole thing and douse them both with lots of coffee.

Coffee may have some side effects, but it's not as bad as whatever else you end up taking. Have you read the warning labels on any of your prescriptions lately? Not that I had planned to operate any heavy machinery anyway. Who is this person who has to be continually warned not to get heavily medicated and then climb onto a forklift?

And I've wondered. Instead of nausea, vomiting, and varying intestinal distresses, why can't they come up with a medication that has a warning label something more like, "may cause extreme kindheartedness and prolonged loving attitude"? You hardly ever see that.

Feed a What, Starve a Where?

I guess it's mostly because a loving attitude is not one of those side effects that just happens. We have to cultivate it. We have to encourage it to grow. Sounds a little moldy but hey, that's how we got penicillin. And it could change the culture—in our churches, outside our churches, and all around them. There's power in the love of God—and in seeing His children love each other—that's world-altering.

In Ephesians 4, we're told to stay alert at guarding our loving unity as believers. We're instructed again and again all through the Word of God to love each other. To love each other with forgiveness. To love each other with sacrificial service. To love each other with generosity, caring for each other's needs. We're told to love each other the way Christ loved us. We're told even further to love each other by coming alongside and helping carry the loads of others. "Bear one another's burdens, and so fulfill the law of Christ" (Galatians 6:2 ESV).

Load-Bearing Laws

Loving each other, coming alongside to help one another—it's not simply a good lifestyle plan. As followers of Christ, it's our law. We have an obligation to love and to climb underneath the heavy load of a friend in trouble.

Comfy? Not so much. But worth it? Oh my, yes!

No one understands bearing another's burdens like our Savior does. He climbed under the impossibly heavy weight of the sin of the world. It was the least comfortable road anyone has ever traveled. He fulfilled the law to offer us grace. Jesus did that out of His great love. Then He told us to love with that same kind of love. In John 13:34, Jesus said, "A new command I give you: Love one another. As I have loved you, so you must love one another." Then again just two chapters later, "My command is this: Love each other as I have loved you," (John 15:12).

His command to love can take us new places in our walk of faith in Christ. So how do we cultivate it? What is our role?

Our Role in Our Growing Culture

Loving in the most "Jesus" ways will very often require something extremely up close and personal from us. Energy when we don't feel it. Time when we don't have it. Compassion and selflessness when we have our own challenges and problems we're dealing with. Yet we were never instructed to love others in their struggles as soon as we felt like it. Or as soon as we could fit it in. Or as soon as all our own struggles were resolved.

As you're willing to step into the difficult, ugly, germy battles of another, you will find that He will provide everything you need so that you can accomplish the task. He will feed you in every way you need to be fed. And He can starve your selfishness every place it needs to die. Energy? He's got it waiting for you. Time? He will provide it for every task you attempt to accomplish in His will. Compassion and selflessness? He will "be" those things in and through you. And as you love another person in the way Christ has called you to, you are fulfilling His law. It's more than a role. It's a command and a calling we can surrender to with joy.

What great blessing there is in that place of surrender—it is well with your soul! Faster than a speeding culture, you find yourself growing in faith like you never imagined. We're starving our flesh and feeding our very soul at every point of surrender. That's cultivating love. And it really will change our culture. I'm in!

Back on My Side of the Planet

Meanwhile, back in Petri-dish City, we're finished with the latest round of the flu bug, and yet I still haven't decided what you're supposed to feed it. I did discover, however, that mine seems to like mocha. That's probably what made me well. I feel so good I'm half tempted to go out and operate some heavy machinery. Just because I can.

 STAYING AWAKE IN HIS WORD

Therefore I, a prisoner for serving the Lord, beg you to lead a life worthy of your calling, for you have been called by God. Always be humble and gentle. Be patient with each other, making allowance for each other's faults because of your love. Make every effort to keep yourselves united in the Spirit, binding yourselves together with peace.

— Ephesians 4:1–3 (NLT)

Watchful,
Wide Awake

This week's discovery: I should never record coffee before my first cup of radio.

Alert to His Coming
— What a Way to Go

> "Therefore be alert, since you don't know
> what day your Lord is coming"
> (MATTHEW 24:42 HCSB).

PEOPLE HAVE TOLD me that I think about coffee too much. What? Honestly, I can't coffee coff in the world they're coffeeing about. Incidentally, I would also like to inform those people that I certainly am not always thinking about coffee.

Because sometimes I think about chocolate. Also mocha.

Chocolatey-choc-choc-choc

Confession. I can put away the chocolate. Anytime I have a big box of chocolates sitting in my pantry and I'm tempted to eat one, I know exactly how to get rid of the temptation. Eat the whole box. Temptation gone. Problem solved.

You know those desserts you see with names like *Death by Chocolate, Killer Cookies, Murderously Decadent Chocolate Cake?* One sniff of any of those and all I can think is, hey, what a way to go.

Hershey, Pennsylvania? I would live there. Fannie May? I'm a fan. And even though Willie Wonka gives me the creeps, I would take a free-sample tour of his factory in a heartbeat. If my husband had let me, I would've named one of my children *Ghirardelli.* I thought about petitioning for *Godiva,* too, but that one seemed wrong even to me.

It seems like every few months someone discovers something new and wonderful chocolate does for us. I'm almost sure someone told me that they now believe it will extend your life, give you greater mental acuity, and bring about world peace. Since they now think chocolate can keep you healthy, and more recently they're saying popcorn is better for you than a boatload of vegetables, I say why not cancel the gym membership and let's all go to the movies?

Nobody Knows the Truffles I've Seen

Of course, there's also a good chance that my thighs are now made of 97 percent chocolate. I love thinking about chocolate but I have to tell you, I do not love the thought of thighs with a gooey chocolate center. I try not to think of my thighs as chubby. I'd prefer to think of them as strongly tethered, trussed, and reinforced with a sort of chocolate Kevlar. In a gun battle, you'll want to take cover behind these thighs.

Some say that chocolate is cheaper than therapy. And with chocolate you hardly ever have to have an appointment.

Do You Have an Appointment?

The truth is, we have a better-than-chocolate future in store for us. There's a place Jesus Himself is preparing. That's something ultra-sweet to think about. There is an appointment. We just don't know exactly when it is. And that's OK. Jesus will come again. He said in Mark 13:32–33 (HCSB), "Now concerning that day or hour no one knows — neither the angels in heaven nor the Son — except the Father. Watch! Be alert! For you don't know when the time is coming."

We don't need to know the time of that appointment. We simply need to rest in the truth that it will happen and to be sure that the Father knows. We need to also understand that the important part to Him is that we're alert — watching, waiting, expecting.

Paul lets us in on the plan in 1 Corinthians 15:51–53 (NLT):

But let me reveal to you a wonderful secret. We will not all die, but we will all be transformed! It will happen in a moment, in the blink of an eye, when the last trumpet is blown. For when the trumpet sounds, those who have died will be raised to live forever. And we who are living will also be transformed. For our dying bodies must be transformed into bodies that will never die; our mortal bodies must be transformed into immortal bodies.

Now there's an appointment I don't want to miss!

Ready or Not

Some of our most enthusiastic calls to stay alert have to do with the second coming of Christ. The Lord wants us to anticipate His coming. He wants us to live alert—knowing that He could appear at any second. Knowing He could come any moment keeps us looking up, watching for Him. It keeps us Jesus-conscious.

Anticipating His coming also has a purifying effect on our lives. When I know someone is coming over, let's face it, I fix myself up a little more determinedly. I'll make sure I'm dressed and have some makeup on. We read in 1 John 3:2–3 (HCSB),

> *Dear friends, we are God's children now, and what we will be has not yet been revealed. We know that when He appears, we will be like Him because we will see Him as He is. And everyone who has this hope in Him purifies himself just as He is pure.*

Knowing He's coming inspires us to keep our lives cleaned up and ready. Jesus said,

> *Behold, I am going to come like a thief! Blessed (happy, to be envied) is he who stays awake (alert) and who guards his clothes, so that he may not be naked and have the shame of being seen exposed!* (REVELATION 16:15 AMP).

Chocolate-Covered Faith Watch

Thinking about coffee and chocolate is OK. There's nothing wrong with anticipating the next mocha either. But where we continually keep our minds will determine how we live. Focusing on the Lord's imminent return affects how we treat others, how urgently we share Christ with them, how we love, how we walk out our faith life—it even affects how we pray. Every time we consider His coming, we should be drawn all the more to prayer, to staying connected to Him. Not because praying will cause us to know when He's coming, but because it will cause us to be ready for His coming.

You can be attentively excited that He could be here any minute. If you've surrendered your life to Christ, He has a glorious future in store for you.

> *In My Father's house are many dwelling places; if not, I would have told you. I am going away to prepare a place for you. If I go away and prepare a place for you, I will come back and receive you to Myself, so that where I am you may be also"* (John 14:2–3 HCSB).

We're not only to be excited by His second coming, but the Bible tells us that His second coming is designed to be a source of comfort. Paul wrote,

> *For the Lord himself will come down from heaven, with a loud command, with the voice of the archangel and with the trumpet call of God, and the dead in Christ will rise first. After that, we who are still alive and are left will be caught up together with them in the clouds to meet the Lord in the air. And so we will be with the Lord forever. Therefore encourage one another with these words"* (1 Thessalonians 4:16–18).

These are words to encourage our hearts.

Piece of Cake

It's easy to get excited. I'm pumped about our amazing future. I'm also OK with getting to heaven according to His plan for me and in His timing, not mine. Despite the fact that a friend is making me a "death by chocolate" cake this week. Because I think that means I could be in critical condition by Thursday.

STAYING AWAKE IN HIS WORD

Listen, I tell you a mystery: We will not all sleep, but we will all be changed — in a flash, in the twinkling of an eye, at the last trumpet. For the trumpet will sound, the dead will be raised imperishable, and we will be changed. For the perishable must clothe itself with the imperishable and the mortal with immortality. When the perishable has been clothed with the imperishable, and the mortal with immortality, then the saying that is written will come true: "Death has been swallowed up in victory."

"Where, O death, is your victory? Where, O death, is your sting?"

The sting of death is sin, and the power of sin is the law. But thanks be to God! He gives us the victory through our Lord Jesus Christ."

— 1 CORINTHIANS 15:51–57

Coffee and me. We've been through a lot together. Now we're co-writing a book.

Alert to the Enemy
— Who's Calling the Shots?

> "Stay alert! Watch out for your great enemy, the devil. He prowls
> around like a roaring lion, looking for someone to devour"
>
> (1 PETER 5:8 NLT).

I'VE NOTICED THAT a lot of us have different coffees for different occasions. There's a party coffee—and you should always add sprinkles to that one. There's a "show your friends you know how to order something trendy and hip at the coffee bar" coffee. You almost have to be a barista for that one. And there's a "curling up in front of the fireplace at home" brew. It's too plain to impress your friends and not fancy enough to capture your attention at the coffee bar. But it's comfy. It's sort of the sweat pants of coffee.

It might be handy if someone came up with a way to read the coffee signals. Wouldn't it be great if they made a Rosetta Stone for deciphering the language of coffee? Or maybe something like "mood coffee." The boss takes it with an extra sweetener this morning? Ask for an extralong lunch. Whipped cream? Maybe it's a good day to ask for that raise. Black and bitter? Not the day to talk about the cappuccino you accidentally spilled into the office copier.

Personally, espresso is my own "throw caution to the wind" drink. Once the caffeine starts talking I can't seem to get a word in edgewise. Who *is* calling the shots?

Sometimes it's the coffee talking. Sometimes it's more about my attitude. Every once in a while, I'll tell somebody that the world is my oyster. What I actually mean is that sometimes it's kind of slimy and smells like fish.

Cheap Shot

The truth is, we do live in a fallen world. It can be slimy here. And we need to be on guard. Take a look at another version of the verse in 1 Peter that heads up this chapter: "Be serious! Be alert! Your adversary the Devil is prowling around like a roaring lion, looking for anyone he can devour" (1 Peter 5:8 HCSB). Satan and his forces of evil are active. They're always on the lookout for ways to trip you up. And they'll take every cheap shot.

So if the enemy is on the attack, how do you fight? The next verse tells us. "Resist him and be firm in the faith" (v. 9 HCSB). The word translated "resist" is the Greek term that means to "stand up against" him. We're not to take this lying down. This is no time to throw our alertness to the wind.

Our weapon in the battle is not what some might expect. What are we to "stand up against" him with? Our firm faith! Ephesians 6 confirms it. The "shield of faith" is part of the armor of God that we're to put on so we can "stand against the devil's schemes." Paul writes that with the shield of faith "you can extinguish all the flaming arrows of the evil one" (Ephesians 6:16).

This is no wimpy shield. Let's think about what faith really is. Faith is a belief and trust in God that results in a changed life—a life surrendered to Him in obedience. Surrender and obedience take us in the exact opposite direction from where our enemy wants us to go. Actively loving and following Christ is resisting the devil.

We also resist by His Word. When Jesus was tempted by Satan, He responded each time with the Word of God. Romans 10:17 (NKJV) says that "faith comes by hearing, and hearing by the word of God." For the faith that saved us in the first place, and for the growing faith that will make us strong and battle-ready, we have to hear, believe, and act on His Word.

Something Fishy

Your adversary will try to deceive you. The Greek word for "devil" in 1 Peter 5:8 is the word "slanderer." Jesus told us that Satan is a liar "and the father of lies" (John 8:44). Everything he wants you to believe is fishy at the very least. He works to convince you that evil is good and good is evil. He wants to lead you to believe that there are other things that deserve your worship more than God. Or he will simply try to distract you from worshipping God with everything shiny. He will try to convince you that Jesus isn't real or that He can't do what He said. He will send you a sneaky message that Jesus won't really change your life or your future. He'll lie to you about God's Word and twist it around as he did with Eve. He'll seek to convince you that obedience is not that big of a deal. Sometimes he tries to distract you from walking by faith by working to convince you that you need to measure up, and that you should focus on doing good works to earn God's favor. Anything to get you to deny God's grace and to chip away at the kind of faith that makes a difference in the kingdom of God.

The enemy will tempt you to sin. The last thing he wants is for you to bear fruit and experience victory in your Christian life. You can bet he'll be working to devour your fruit. And your reputation. And your witness.

But listen. Never think for a minute that the evil one is calling the shots here. We have the victory. Done deal. Not in our own strength, but as we stay alert to the enemy and his schemes and stand firm in our faith and submit to the Lord, He will be our strength. He is our devil resistance. James 4:7 says, "Submit yourselves, then, to God. Resist the devil, and he will flee from you." Surrendering to the Father. It's the key. It sends the enemy running.

He runs. We stand.

Parting Shot

I truly do want to live a life of victory. It helps to focus on where I'm headed. This world may have its slimy parts, but it's encouraging to remember that this oyster is not my home. Living in espresso-flavored alertness—it might even prove to be higher in omega 3s. And with no fishy aftertaste.

STAYING AWAKE IN HIS WORD

Finally, be strong in the Lord and in his mighty power. Put on the full armor of God, so that you can take your stand against the devil's schemes. For our struggle is not against flesh and blood, but against the rulers, against the authorities, against the powers of this dark world and against the spiritual forces of evil in the heavenly realms. Therefore put on the full armor of God, so that when the day of evil comes, you may be able to stand your ground, and after you have done everything, to stand. Stand firm then, with the belt of truth buckled around your waist, with the breastplate of righteousness in place, and with your feet fitted with the readiness that comes from the gospel of peace. In addition to all this, take up the shield of faith, with which you can extinguish all the flaming arrows of the evil one. Take the helmet of salvation and the sword of the Spirit, which is the word of God.

— EPHESIANS 6:10–17

I've begged it, jiggled it, banged on it —
still nothing from my coffee maker. It's official.
The thing is dead. Go to Def Con 2.

13

Alert to Hope
— Hope Springs Internal

"Therefore, preparing your minds for action, and being sober-minded, set your hope fully on the grace that will be brought to you at the revelation of Jesus Christ" (1 PETER 1:13 ESV).

COFFEE DOESN'T REALLY make the world go round. But I think it's very possible it makes the trip more pleasant. Keeping a sense of humor about the whole thing probably doesn't hurt either.

I was asked about my sense of humor by a couple of radio show hosts recently. They asked if it had developed and grown over the years. I think they were wondering if I did something to deserve this or if it just sort of warped this way on its own. Maybe they were trying to somehow make sure it never happened to them. Anyway, I started thinking about my humor history.

I realized I liked being the class clown when getting one of my first laughs in first grade with the classic, "Say wagon. Your pants are draggin'." The stuff of legends, that was. I was using someone else's material, but still.

I matured by second grade with an equally critically acclaimed, yet more contemporary for the time, "We-e-e-e-ll, doggies!" I sounded so much like Jed Clampett it was scary. By third grade I realized Roger Miller had gotten more mileage out of the rhyme joke than the basic wagon/draggin'. I thought the poetry in one of his songs was epic. Remember this one? "Roses are red. Violets are purple. Sugar's sweet and so is maple surple."

So I decided to try my hand at it with this not nearly so acclaimed ditty: "Roses are red. Violets are blue. Rhyming is hard. But hey, look! I got Pixie Stix . . . and *Batman* is on!" In retrospect I'm pretty sure I was at least a little ADD.

Historical or Hysterical

It's interesting to look at your own history. But we've also been told to keep our eyes focused forward. We're not to get so hung up on the past that we miss what's happening now and what's in store for our future.

Paul said in Philippians 3:13–14, "One thing I do: Forgetting what is behind and straining toward what is ahead, I press on toward the goal to win the prize for which God has called me heavenward in Christ Jesus."

When we're looking forward, we're reminded of the glorious future we have because of Christ. That gives us the most beautiful hope. First Peter 1:3–4 (HCSB) says,

> *Praise the God and Father of our Lord Jesus Christ. According to His great mercy, He has given us a new birth in a living hope through the resurrection of Jesus Christ from the dead and into an inheritance that is imperishable, uncorrupted, and unfading, kept in heaven for you.*

In our society, we use the word *hope* a little differently than this hope of the New Testament. "I hope the coffee is hot." "I hope I get that job." "I hope I get to retire from that job." I hope there's chocolate at the meeting." "I hope we don't have the meeting." "I hope I meet the person of my dreams soon." "I hope he'll stop calling." Most people have a "hope-so" kind of hope—one with a meaning closer to "wish" than hope. There's always an air of uncertainty connected to it.

From the Inside Out

The hope of a believer in Christ—real hope—has nothing to do with rubbing some sort of magic lamp. It's not a wish. It's a knowing. A sure, unshakable knowledge anchored in a powerful Savior. No wishing. No uncertainty. That's because it's a "living hope," according to 1 Peter 1:3.

Jesus rose from the dead. He is living. And by His Holy Spirit, He lives within each of us. So where does that put the hope? Right inside us! Paul said in Romans 15:13, "May the God of hope fill you with all joy and peace as you trust in him, so that you may overflow with hope by the power of the Holy Spirit." We're filled with hope because we're filled with Him. He's alive and working that hope, bringing joy and peace right along with it. It's hope that overflows!

True hope is found as we understand that every time we rest our hopes in ourselves and what we can accomplish, we end up frustrated and hopeless. We grab onto true hope when we realize that hope is only secure as it rests firmly in Jesus. Never try to fill in yourself what can only be filled by Christ.

Hope at the End of Your Rope

Even as believers, we can forget what we have. Ever feel like you're at the end of your rope—hopeless? I want you to know, there's renewed hope for you. As a matter of fact, there's a special hope for you when you're at the end of your rope. Sometimes coming to the end of your rope is coming to the end of yourself. It's there that we allow the Lord to strip away our pride and we get out of the way of what God wants to accomplish in us.

Self-sufficiency is the enemy of hope. Paul said in Philippians 4:13 (AMP), "I am ready for anything and equal to anything through Him Who infuses inner strength into me, that is, I am self-sufficient in Christ's sufficiency."

Get to the end of yourself and you'll find hope there. In Jesus' parable of the prodigal son, the straying son comes to a place of revelation:

There was a man who had two sons. The younger one said to his father, "Father, give me my share of the estate." So he divided his property between them. Not long after that, the younger son got together all he had, set off for a distant country and there squandered his wealth in wild living. After he had spent everything, there was a severe famine in that whole country, and he began to be in need. So he went and hired himself out to a citizen of that country, who sent him to his fields to feed pigs. He longed to fill his stomach with the pods that the pigs were eating, but no one gave him anything. When he came to his senses, he said, "How many of my father's hired men have food to spare, and here I am starving to death!" . . . So he got up and went to his father. But while he was still a long way off, his father saw him and was filled with compassion for him; he ran to his son, threw his arms around him and kissed him (LUKE 15:11–17, 20).

The son came to his senses when he got to the end of his rope — the end of himself. One of the most astounding, grace-filled, hope-giving scenes in all of God's Word to me is the one where we get to picture that father running to the son. He embraced him, restored him, showed him mercy and amazing love.

Keep holding onto the rope and what do you end up with? Rope. But let go and you'll find yourself holding onto a hope you may never even have imagined.

Always keep in mind that ours is not a "hope for the best" kind of hope. It's more like: Hope! For the best — is already ours!

Prose and Cons

I would put that in poetry form, but we all know the ADD could send us in a very bad prose direction. Although I did share my third grade poem with one hopeful friend who said that maybe it's just that I was free verse before free verse was cool.

STAYING AWAKE IN HIS WORD

I pray that the eyes of your heart may be enlightened in order that you may know the hope to which he has called you, the riches of his glorious inheritance in his holy people, and his incomparably great power for us who believe. That power is the same as the mighty strength he exerted when he raised Christ from the dead and seated him at his right hand in the heavenly realms.

— EPHESIANS 1:18–20

I can rise. And I can shine. But should anyone really expect me to do both at the same time without coffee?

14

Alert to Grace
— Venti, Vidi, Vici

"So brace up your minds; be sober . . . morally alert; set your hope wholly and unchangeably on the grace (divine favor) that is coming to you"
(1 PETER 1:13 AMP).

COFFEE-SPEAK CAN SOMETIMES be tough to interpret. Even the sizes of the cups are in code. Short? Tall? Aren't those heights? *Grande? Venti?* Really? I was trying to order the other day and finally just came out with something like, "*Veni, vidi, venti.*"

I'm pretty sure I meant: "I came, I saw, I ordered a large coffee."

Next I was staring at the menu—a long list of beverages and brews in every bean and blend. *Oy vey.* What to choose from the mega list? I needed coffee before I could order my coffee. On top of that, the menu list brought to mind the giant to-do list in my purse. Another *oy.* Another *vey.* It was only right that I considered upping the size of my coffee at that point.

How about: "*Veni, vidi, VAT!*"—meaning "just give me a VAT of coffee and I'll move along without making a scene, thank you."

Do you have mornings like that one, when there doesn't seem to be even the remotest possibility you'll have enough coffee to rightly correspond to the size of your to-do list?

To Do or Not to Do

If extreme list-making were a sport, I could be an Olympian. I have actually caught myself making lists of my lists. Is this a sport or an illness? It's interesting to me that if it's ever classified as a disorder and they come up with a 12-step program for it, they'll have to *list* the steps.

One of my favorite things about lists is checking. That might sound Olympic-sport-related, but it's really about making that magical checkmark. One more item off the list. I love that. Most of the time, I'll put a couple of things on my list that I've already done—just so I can check them off.

Wake up? Check. Drink coffee? Check. And check. And usually before noon, another check.

Some people are "list people" because they're organized. I'm a list person because I'm not organized. I forget, or somehow manage to mess up most everything I don't write down.

Backlist

You know what's amazing? Despite my long, long list of mess-ups—of every size and flavor—God's grace is still there, unchanging. No matter what. As a matter of fact, there's not a single thing I can put on my list of failures that His grace can't cross right off the list. Not a check. A Cross.

Never think for a second that God's grace isn't big enough for a sin you've committed. No need to keep a backlog of failures in your mind. If you've confessed and forsaken a sin, grace is yours because of the Cross. And that's big enough. Could you possibly look at your sin and say to yourself, "No, the death of Jesus was not enough for this one." His sacrifice was complete. His grace will cover you, clean you, get you back on track. His forgiveness, His mercy—they're yours. Grasping the depth of His grace is a tall order for sure. Think *überventi*. Then bigger. Then infinitely bigger than that.

Saving Grace, Seasoning Grace, Sustaining Grace

It Saves Us! We can't earn grace or it's no longer grace. "For it is by grace you have been saved, through faith—and this is not from yourselves, it is the gift of God—not by works, so that no one can boast" (Ephesians 2:8–9). If you have given your life to Christ, your sin has been thoroughly erased through the gift of His grace.

It Seasons Us! Then once we're saved, we continue to live in that grace. It's His grace that changes us, grows us, seasons us. It doesn't add duties so that we can live up to our salvation. It's a change of purpose because of a change of heart. He transforms our desires, our thoughts, our words, and our actions. That's more of His grace at work. "He has saved us and called us to a holy life—not because of anything we have done but because of his own purpose and grace. This grace was given us in Christ Jesus before the beginning of time" (2 Timothy 1:9).

It Sustains Us! He also gives us comforting grace for trials we face. It's the kind of grace that holds us up when circumstances are difficult and when life is painful. When Paul was in pain, the Lord told him, "My grace is sufficient for you" (2 Corinthians 12:9). There it is again—the "enough-ness" of His grace. It's everything we need.

Grace by the Vat!

Just when you think there couldn't possibly be more, there's more grace still. "For from his fullness we have all received, grace upon grace" (John 1:16 ESV). So I'm thinking about the grace of God today and His great love for me. I'm thinking about that grace upon grace, my heart overflowing with gratitude. You can bask in that grace too. Know that it's yours. Do you want a stronger faith? Second Timothy 2:1 says to "be strong in the grace that is in Christ Jesus." If you're searching for strength, look toward His grace.

Let's set a goal to make staying alert to that amazing grace a part of every day's to-do list.

Me? I'll probably get to stay alert to it well into the night, too—since I don't' think I'll be sleeping. A few too many check marks by the "drink coffee" thing.

STAYING AWAKE IN HIS WORD

But God, who is rich in mercy, because of His great love that He had for us, made us alive with the Messiah even though we were dead in trespasses. You are saved by grace! Together with Christ Jesus He also raised us up and seated us in the heavens, so that in the coming ages He might display the immeasurable riches of His grace through His kindness to us in Christ Jesus. For you are saved by grace through faith, and this is not from yourselves; it is God's gift — not from works, so that no one can boast.

— EPHESIANS 2:4–9 (HCSB)

What time is it? Oh yeah, it's about half past shoulda-already-had-a-second-cup-of-coffee.

Alert to Temptation
— Tempted and Tried, Keep Wide the Stride

"Stay alert; be in prayer so you
don't wander into temptation without
even knowing you're in danger"
(MATTHEW 26:40 *THE MESSAGE*).

MY HUSBAND WENT shopping with me the other day. He was just like a kid in a candy store. A kid who never ever wants to eat candy. Or see candy. Or be near candy. Ever.

Still, I love it when Richie goes with me. He's so happy to stop, sit, and share a cup of coffee. It's because he'll do anything to put the shopping on pause . . . but still.

Not only is there some sweet coffee time on those trips, but once we're back in shopping gear if there's an item that tickles my fancy, I just hold it up and ask him what he thinks. Richie: "If I say we can buy it, will we be any closer to going home?" I come home with more great stuff that way.

When I'm shopping alone, there's almost always this annoying little voice of sensibility to deal with. "You don't really need that necklace, you know." Goofy voice. I try to reason with it. "Are you kidding me? This necklace is perfect for that new outfit. I don't have anything that goes with that." The voice will usually come back with something smug and snarky like, "If you remember, I told you not to buy that either." Goofy, goofy voice.

Oh, It's On

I do have a backup battle plan. I know the voice well. It's got weaknesses. I can usually shut it down when I pull out the argument to end all arguments. It's those four most magical words: "But it's on sale!"

A few weeks ago I was shopping alone when a cute top caught my eye. I think it may have winked at me. I stood there and watched as the top and that little voice started to rumble. "I'm on sale," it said to the voice. The voice fired back in a condescending tone, "You're purple, orange, and yellow, for Pete's sake."

After a pretty heated battle, I sat in the dressing room and watched as the shirt viciously forced itself into my hands and justified it to the voice with, "I'm the only one *and* I'm in her size. It's a sign." Wow, won the battle with force and sounded spiritual doing it. The top was good. Next thing I knew I was wearing it.

Walk, Stand, Sit, Wear

I was reading in the first chapter of Psalms a few days later and it occurred to me that it's oh so similar with sin. "Blessed is the one who does not walk in step with the wicked or stand in the way that sinners take or sit in the company of mockers" (Psalm 1:1).

First walking, then standing, then taking a seat. At first we're just shopping, strolling past the wicked. Maybe we catch a glimpse of something on TV or hear something inappropriate at the office. Or maybe there's a thought that unexpectedly winks its way into our minds. Suddenly we find ourselves standing and listening. We know we should keep walking, but we convince ourselves that giving in for a few minutes couldn't hurt. The next thing we know, the sin is ours. We're pulling up a chair, sitting down, getting comfortable with it. Wearing it.

We may try to convince ourselves we were taken by force, but we've actually made every choice along the way. We've chosen to buy the sin and to put it on.

There's a way to stop the process. Keep on walking. You can keep on walking as you pray, as you focus your life on bringing glory to the name of your God and as you plant your face in His Word. Staying rooted and grounded in His Word doesn't "tempt-proof" a life, but it helps equip that life for victory over temptation. His Word is key. Every time Jesus was tempted of Satan, He responded with the Word. As we read, study, meditate on, and memorize His Word and let it permeate our thinking, our minds become ready to respond according to that Word when a temptation pops up. That's the ticket to walking in step with the Savior instead of walking "in step with the wicked" as Psalm 1:1 puts it. The blessing we think we might find when we're winking back at sin? It's deceptive and doesn't last. The next verse in that psalm tells us that the blessing is reserved for the one "whose delight is in the law of the LORD" (Psalm 1:2). The voice of reason is His voice as He instructs us in victorious living through His Word.

Un-sit, Unplug, Un-sin

As you resolve to keep on walking, it's wise to see to some practical details. If there are temptations that especially hound you—areas where you know you're vulnerable—don't make a place for those things in your life. Don't sit still and welcome the battle. In any battle it's good to know your enemy's weaknesses. Satan is your enemy, yes. But sometimes your enemy is just plain you. You certainly don't want the devil teaming up with your flesh for the double whammy. Paul says in Ephesians 4:27 (HCSB), "Don't give the Devil an opportunity."

Bottom line, every place you can avoid temptation, do. I joke about shopping, but if unwise or ungodly spending is a temptation for you, don't spend hours poring over a catalog or Internet site. Don't stroll through the mall just for fun or turn on the shopping channel that you know will fuel your wants. If you're tempted to go in an ungodly direction in other areas on the Internet, unplug when you're alone. Make yourself accountable to a family member or a trusted friend. If certain movies or TV shows cause your thoughts to head in a wrong direction, unplug there too.

Are there places you allow yourself to "stroll by"—places you know could lead you to standing for a wrong cause or sitting in a place of sin? Make a 180 and head in the opposite direction. Let every victory over temptation help you with the next. Let each be a lesson in how to focus on Christ and keep on walking.

I get an extra little "keep on walking" lesson every time I wear that top. It's purple, yellow, and orange, for real. With a touch of leopard-print trim, no less. And don't think for a second that voice doesn't gloat.

 STAYING AWAKE IN HIS WORD

When tempted, no one should say, "God is tempting me." For God cannot be tempted by evil, nor does he tempt anyone; but each person is tempted when they are dragged away by their own evil desire and enticed. Then, after desire has conceived, it gives birth to sin; and sin, when it is full-grown, gives birth to death.

— JAMES 1:13–15

OK, you know those forms that ask for your emergency contact information?
I think I'm going to start putting the coffee shop on mine.

Alert to the Needs of Others
— What Gives?

> "Pay attention and always be on your guard —
> looking out for one another"
> (LUKE 17:3 AMP).

FOR EVERYTHING YOU can name, I'm pretty sure there's an official phobia listed for it. If you're afraid of phobias, would you be considered a *phob-a-phobe*? I'm not sure if it's official, but some have even claimed there's a *javaphobia* — fear of coffee. Weird. The only coffee phobia I could almost relate to was the fear of forgetting to turn on the coffeemaker and waking up coffeeless. *Folger's-phobia*. Which is somewhere between very weird and very funny.

I'm not sure how true it is, but it's noted in several places that there are surveys showing the fear of public speaking (*glossophobia*) and the fear of dying (*necrophobia*) at the top of people's lists of most dreaded fears. In that order even.

As a public speaker — and one who is often billed as a humorist — I think tops on my list would be "*necro-glosso-phobia.*" Death while speaking. OK, yes, I made that one up. But I've experienced it on a figurative level once or twice. Now that's a frightening event.

When Crickets Chirp

One of those events particularly sticks in my mind. I was animatedly delivering what I considered some of my most rip-roaring material when . . . it happened: nothing. A whole big lot of nothing. Hardly a snicker. I think I may have heard crickets chirping. Kind of a slow death, speaker-wise. The Bible says that laughter is like medicine. I'm telling you, this crowd had to be the control group. Placebos for everyone!

It's good for me to remember, though, that I can't always tell what people are feeling on the inside. After that same event where I experienced the excessive and painful cricket-chirping, a lady came up to me with a completely lifeless face. Truly lifeless. I was hoping she wasn't going to need CPR. Without an ounce of expression, she mono-toned, "I have never laughed so hard in all my life." Not a smile even.

I can't even begin to tell you how hard I had to fight falling over in slobbering laughter right there on the spot.

Check Your Vitals

Here's hoping we always look "alive" to the world. Know what "alive" looks like? It looks like love. First John 3:14 says, "We know that we have passed from death to life, because we love our brothers."

We have passed from death into life—heavy on the life! We need to pass it on. Others can't see our redemption unless we live it out. And love it out.

It's not a new message, but it's one we need to hear often. We read in the same passage, "This is the message you heard from the beginning: We should love one another" (1 John 3:11). It's a message clearly worth repeating: Love is vital. Staying alert to the needs of others? Vital. So how do we know exactly what that kind of love alertness is supposed to look like? The same chapter gives us that, too: "This is how we know what love is: Jesus Christ laid down his life for us. And we ought to lay down our lives for our brothers" (v.16).

Real love sacrifices. The Jesus kind of love is a love that surrenders in humility. It's a love that endures beyond the very worst offenses. Hebrews 13:16 (ESV) says, "Do not neglect to do good and to share what you have, for such sacrifices are pleasing to God."

Live Alert

When Jesus was asked which commandment in the law was greatest, He answered, "Love the Lord your God with all your heart and with all your soul and with all your mind. This is the first and greatest commandment. And the second is like it: 'Love your neighbor as yourself'" (Matthew 22:37–39). A right-to-the-heart-and-soul kind of love. Being a follower of Christ means we love Him with everything we've got, and we love others in His name with the same enthusiastic love. It's our focus. Because it's God's focus.

That kind of loving alertness to the needs of others includes giving generously. What gives? We do! God's Word lets us know that giving is good for us in every way.

> *Give freely and become more wealthy; be stingy and lose everything. The generous will prosper; those who refresh others will themselves be refreshed. People curse those who hoard their grain, but they bless the one who sells in time of need* (PROVERBS 11:24–26 NLT).

We should give out of love for the Lord but blessing, sometimes even our own monetary blessing, comes as we generously give to others. Everything works miraculously different in God's economy.

Look Alive!

Here's hoping that if I'm asked to lay aside my rights, my fears, my possessions, my pride, even my very life for another, I'll give the right response. No silence. No crickets chirping. Just love. If I'm honest, I'll admit that there are times I'm not even willing to give up my parking spot for another. *O Lord, keep me alert to the needs of others. Give me the ability to love as You do!*

I can't really tell what an audience is feeling on the inside. We can't really tell what people are feeling on the inside in any set of circumstances either. We do know that there are so many who are downright heartsick. Whatever they're experiencing, let's just love them. Let's meet their needs whenever we can—all because we love and serve Christ. Let's look alive!

Giving sacrificial love to a heartsick world that doesn't know the love and joy of Jesus is the best medicine we can offer. And that, my friends, is no placebo.

STAYING AWAKE IN HIS WORD

Do nothing from factional motives [through contentiousness, strife, selfishness, or for unworthy ends] or prompted by conceit and empty arrogance. Instead, in the true spirit of humility (lowliness of mind) let each regard the others as better than and superior to himself [thinking more highly of one another than you do of yourselves]. Let each of you esteem and look upon and be concerned for not [merely] his own interests, but also each for the interests of others.

— PHILIPPIANS 2:3–4 AMP

How can they say coffee is addictive?
I'm not addicted and I drink it every single day.

Alert to Forgiveness
— What's Your Grind?

> "Be alert. If you see your friend going wrong,
> correct him. If he responds, forgive him"
> (LUKE 17:3 *THE MESSAGE*).

WHENEVER I FLY, a tall low-fat mocha with extra whip is my personal fuel of choice. I fly the friendly skies a lot friendlier with a cup of that particular friendliness in my hand—even though the coffee lines at the airport are killer.

Last time, I was 20 minutes in a long coffee line and still the lady in front of me waited to decide what to order until she got to the register. Really, Lady? She spent about half of that time asking questions about the grind, then the next half trying to decide whether to froth or not to froth. I was grinding a little myself—and working up a bit of a personal froth while I was at it. I thought I should probably get bonus spiritual points, though, when she looked back at me and I decided to smile. There may have been a bit of snark to the smile, but still. Kindness sort of won out.

I'm now going to give you a helpful suggestion. If you ever try killing someone with kindness, try not to look disappointed when you find out they don't actually die. OK, I'm just kidding. Mostly.

It all made me long for my own coffee pot back at home, my favorite mug. Maybe even a piece of toast.

Pop Quiz
Lately, though, I've noticed weird things popping up out of my toaster back at home. A banana split? Didn't see that coming. Who knew toaster

tarts were popping up with flavors like Chocolate Banana Split? No kidding. Even Chocolate Chip Cookie Dough. My teens love them, but my adult taste buds haven't been too impressed.

The real question is: Is there really any way to make a cookie-covered toaster-breakfast taste like a chocolate banana split? Personally, I'd rather have the chocolate banana split for breakfast instead.

The real thing is so much better. And it hardly ever burns.

We're Toast

When was the last time someone burned you a bit? Is there somebody you want to have for breakfast? And I'm not talking about offering them a pastry. Does a face pop up in your mind? How we respond when we're hurt has a huge impact on our walk of faith. If we get frothed up and ready to explode, we're not responding in faith. If we keep it to ourselves and harbor secret bitterness instead, hanging on to unforgiveness, we're still not responding in faith. It's like we're all frothed up with nowhere to go.

Failing to forgive is a destructive choice for a follower of Christ. It's destructive to relationships and it's destructive for that very follower. Paul writes in Colossians 3:13 (ESV), "bearing with one another and, if one has a complaint against another, forgiving each other; as the Lord has forgiven you, so you also must forgive."

When someone commits an offense against you and the hurt runs deep, forgiveness isn't always the easy choice. Sometimes everything within us—our selfish flesh—will tell us it's time to retaliate. Your selfishness and anger can work together to convince you that revenge is the only way to make it right. But revenge is like giving your enemy a missile launcher and painting a target on your own back. It will explode in bitterness that can find its way into every corner of your life.

We're called to forgive as we've been forgiven. We have to make that choice. When we do, we're choosing the way of peace instead of projectiles. When we don't, we're toast.

Don't Go Ballistic

Forgiveness is about more than getting rid of the destructive results of bitterness. It's your God-directed obligation to willingly give up your resentment toward someone who has hurt you. It's choosing not to hold on to it, and not to try to get even. It's more than just saying the words, "I forgive you." Forgiveness is a release that happens in the heart. When you don't make the choice to forgive, bitterness takes root. It spreads like a weed sending shoots into your heart and your character, choking out every good thing your heavenly Father wants to do.

Just as forgiveness is a choice we make, unforgiveness is a choice as well. We can convince ourselves it's the person who hurt us who caused the resulting misery but, in truth, we've lit the fuse on that cannon ourselves. Never underestimate the deadly, miserable, tragic effects of bitterness. Our worship gets stuck. Our prayer life is put on hold. The fire of our witness is snuffed out. We can't enjoy our relationship with the Father or with other people. It loads extra conflict and stress onto our spirit and our body that can actually cause illness. Mocha doesn't even taste as good. There's hardly a thing we love in life that bitterness can't poison.

Let Kindness Truly Win Out

So what do we do? First, acknowledge unforgiveness as sin. Confess it as the ugly offense it is and ask the Lord to forgive you. Then choose to walk away from the unforgiveness. In Ephesians 4:32 the Apostle Paul writes, "Be kind and compassionate to one another, forgiving each other, just as in Christ God forgave you." When your selfishness screams, "I have rights!" "I didn't deserve this!" "I've been hurt!" tell your selfishness that the Lord forgave you. He had rights. He didn't deserve it. He'd been hurt. And the Father continues to forgive you. Just as you must continue to forgive others.

When you sense those ugly feelings creeping back into your mind and heart, don't let them set a trap for you there that will drag you back into bitterness. Don't rehearse the person's offense again in your mind or give imaginary speeches you think that person needs to hear. Every time you're tempted to replay it in your mind, discipline yourself to pray for your offender. You'll see God do a miraculous healing in your spirit—sometimes instantly. Sometimes over a longer time as the Father works in your heart to build character and consistency and full reliance on Him for everything you need to keep on forgiving.

Getting rid of bitterness makes room in your heart for you to receive blessing. Getting rid of resentment makes a place for joy. Emptying out hate leaves room for peace and love. By the power of God, you can be free to walk victoriously in faith—maybe like never before.

I don't know about you, but when the heat is on, I want to pop up by faith—all in His power—ready to forgive and grow. More with the growth. Less with the froth.

STAYING AWAKE IN HIS WORD

Do not repay anyone evil for evil. Be careful to do what is right in the eyes of everyone. If it is possible, as far as it depends on you, live at peace with everyone. Do not take revenge, my dear friends, but leave room for God's wrath, for it is written: "It is mine to avenge; I will repay," says the Lord. On the contrary: "If your enemy is hungry, feed him; if he is thirsty, give him something to drink. In doing this, you will heap burning coals on his head." Do not be overcome by evil, but overcome evil with good.

— ROMANS 12:17–21

*If it's true that coffee can harm your memory,
then I wonder what coffee does.*

18

Alert to a Life Change
— Something to Write Home About

"Oh, what joy for those whose disobedience is forgiven,
whose sin is put out of sight!"
(PSALM 32:1 NLT).

ONE OF THE greatest things about being a writer is that it's a job that comes with a lot of coffee. I can usually get a chapter and a half per cup. More with espresso, but it's usually all one sentence with no punctuation.

I've heard that 86 percent of Americans want to write a book. That surprised me. Although I have heard that most people see writing a book as an adventure. Or maybe they just want to write for the coffee, who knows? I have a tiny bit of perspective to offer, so approximately 86 percent of you should keep on reading.

Now that I've written nine books I'm just starting to learn a few things about the adventure. OK, let's think about it. Your average action/ adventure/spy/hero-type guys can show you the scars from their whip marks, holes from a gunshot wound or two and maybe the disfiguring marks from where they got run over by a tank. Writers? We get to show people the scars from our carpel tunnel surgeries. They get car chases. We get to tell people about that one time a wheel fell off the office chair. Not a lot to write home about.

Where Is Your Home?
The writing life can feel a little remote sometimes. There aren't a lot of people connections sandwiched between the writer and the manuscript.

Sometimes solitude is not so bad. Sometimes it feels more like isolation and it's downright unpleasant.

It's so much worse, though, when we're talking about an isolation from the God of the universe—the creation separated from the Creator. We were created to connect with Him. He knit us together with a longing to have our soul completed in Him and connected to Him. Living a life separated from the heavenly Father will always leave a person feeling like something vital is missing. Because it is.

Even with the awareness of that missing "something," there's a barrier there, standing in the way of getting it. Sin. We've broken God's law. Our God is holy and can't be in the presence of sin and Romans 3:23 says that we all have it. "For all have sinned and fall short of the glory of God." Since God is holy and just, that sin has to be dealt with. How? Death. Romans 6:23 tells us that "the wages of sin" (what we earn for sin) "is death."

Home, Sweet Home

What a sad predicament we would be in if the story ended there. But there's more to the story. There's more to write home about. And there's more to Romans 6:23: "but the gift of God is eternal life in Christ Jesus our Lord." In His mercy, love, and grace, God solved the problem by sending His Son, Jesus, to pay our sin debt. Jesus took care of those "wages" we earned when He took upon Himself our sin and died the degrading death of the Cross. Because He took our place and took our punishment, we are no longer condemned. There's no judgment for our wrongs—all because of Christ. Romans 8:1 (ESV) tells us, "There is therefore now no condemnation for those who are in Christ Jesus."

Three days after Jesus' sacrificial death on the Cross, He rose again, victorious over sin and death. When we ask the Lord to forgive our sin and we fully give our lives to Christ, we give our life to a risen, living Savior!

This amazing gift of salvation is available to anyone who believes in Jesus and what He did and who receives the gift. There's a very satisfied, "at home" sense that comes along with the gift. The "something missing" becomes the piece of the puzzle that actually changes the entire puzzle.

Asking Christ to take control of your life begins a faith walk. Developing a growing, vibrant faith will require blazing some new trails and forming some new habits. But the person who truly gives all to Christ has a new passion to serve the Lord wherever He leads and in whatever capacity He directs.

Run Home
Have you received the gift? If you haven't, why not let today be the day you permanently fill that "something missing." Run home! You can pray right now.
- Acknowledge your sin before your holy God. Confess.
- Tell the Father that you believe that Jesus Christ came to pay for that sin and to grant you the righteousness you couldn't muster up on your own.
- Thank Him for that payment for your sin and for the glorious resurrection of Christ from the dead.
- Ask Him to forgive your sin, to come into your life and to lead you from this moment forward.
- Thank Him for your new life of faith.

If you just prayed giving Jesus your life, let me encourage you to share that with someone. Connect with another believer who can answer some of your questions and help you get started in your new walk of faith. Plug in to a Bible-believing church where you can learn, receive encouragement, and serve the way the Lord calls you to. And may I also tell you that receiving Christ is a no-regrets kind of decision. Your entire destiny has changed and you're embarking on a great adventure.

Close to Home
It's an adventure where we follow hard after Him. When we trust in Jesus, His Holy Spirit makes our hearts His home. He promises to give us strength, wisdom, guidance, joy—everything we genuinely need. Nothing we've deserved, but by His grace and in His love and mercy, everything we need. Rest in that grace and love and mercy and you'll find

yourself enjoying marvelously gratifying faith and a delightfully sweet fellowship with your Creator. Truly, there's no place like home.

 STAYING AWAKE IN HIS WORD

Out of sheer generosity he put us in right standing with himself. A pure gift. He got us out of the mess we're in and restored us to where he always wanted us to be. And he did it by means of Jesus Christ. God sacrificed Jesus on the altar of the world to clear that world of sin. Having faith in him sets us in the clear.

— ROMANS 3:24–25 (*THE MESSAGE*)

Coffee never has unrealistic expectations of me in a morning. Coffee understands me.

Alert to the Devastation of Sin — Faith That Digs In

19

> "There's nobody living right, not even one,
> nobody who knows the score, nobody alert for God"
> (ROMANS 3:9 *THE MESSAGE*).

I HAD ONE of those mornings today. But by the time I'd finished my first cup, I could tell I already had a better coffee-tude. I was thinking this might be the day for a firm regimen of continuous coffee therapy.

It didn't help that earlier in the morning I found . . . and I'm not sure how to tell you this part without being exceedingly gross so I guess I just have to come right out with it. I found what appeared to be fossilized cat barf under the ottoman in my living room. I almost "came right out with it," all right. See, this is why I'll never be a paleontologist. Well, that and also I'm not smart enough, but also that other thing.

After I shuddered off the initial rush of disgust, I will admit to being a little fascinated. I had to wonder what kind of a *hurl-a-saurus* it was. *Ptero-gag-tyl* maybe? *Regurg-a-raptor*?

Digging Up Some Truth

Whatever the fossil record at home reveals though, I do want to be careful in my spiritual life. You don't have to go to the prehistoric data to find that sin can be so stinkin' sneaky. And utterly devastating. You can bet it's easy to find it creeping into your thought patterns. Sometimes we listen to what the world says so often and for so long, it starts to sound right. We can lose sight of its devastation. Not simply the devastation it is to our own lives, but the devastating cost of sin to our Savior.

Coming face to face with the ugliness of your sin is anything but pleasant. It's foul. It's humiliating. Yes, devastating. But necessary. Has it happened to you? It goes something like this:

You get a glimpse of your sin, you look a little more closely at your depravity and your surprising penchant for evil and how you've so often nonchalantly deceived even your own heart about your sinfulness. The revelation is heartrending. Then you weep: mourning, lamenting your wickedness and the idea that you could even be so treacherous.

That's when Jesus comes alongside you. You realize all the more your desperate inability to lift the tiniest finger to fix the miserable situation. And you realize anew your utter dependence on your Savior to do it. It's usually then that in your mind's eye, you glance up at the Cross, and you see your Savior there—bleeding, suffering a humiliating death. There's a sorrow that's almost unbearable. And then there's pain beyond even that. It's the pain of recognizing that His agony should have been yours.

Die to Sin, Live to Faith

We can never forget the Cross. It ever reminds us of what sin does—and is a reminder to stay away from it. God doesn't want us to get complacent. He doesn't want us to be content with just our salvation. He wants more for us. To get in on the "more" we have to die to self, die to sin, and live out our faith in His victory.

Sin is a part of life on this planet. We don't have to dig far to find it. The payment Jesus made for our sin means we have an entirely different future in store—one in which we enjoy with delight the presence of our God instead of the punishment we earned. On this side of heaven though, we will still battle our natural bent to do wrong—our flesh. God wants us to keep a short account of sin. As soon as we see a sin pop up in our lives, we need to confess it and turn away from it. "If we confess our sins, He is faithful and righteous to forgive us our sins and to cleanse us from all unrighteousness" (1 John 1:9 HCSB). Burying sins instead of confessing them can result in the worst kind of fossil situations. Unconfessed sin hinders our fellowship with Him—it cuts us off.

God's grace covers every sin, yes, but His grace is not a "get-out-of-sin-free" permit. Paul said in Romans 6:1–2 (NLT), "Well then, should we keep on sinning so that God can show us more and more of his wonderful grace? Of course not! Since we have died to sin, how can we continue to live in it?" Stretching the truth or outright lying, negative thoughts or attitudes, selfish manipulation of others, hurtful or thoughtless words, pride, lust, greed—those are all things that don't fit in the faith-life of the believer who wants to follow after Christ. He has set us free, for us to finally be able to do the right thing.

Uncovering More Truth

OK, so sometimes I get up in the morning oh so determined to do the right thing. And then I see that there are just so many other options. Sigh. There's another big truth to uncover here. My obedience simply can't be based on my determination. Not in my willpower. Not in anything I can come up with. You either. In one respect, this is not even our fight. It's His.

That's a good thing because He has all power to finish it. We must rely on His Holy Spirit. As we're yielding to Him, stepping out in obedience to His leadings, even when sinful desires creep in and seem absolutely overwhelming, we find that through the Spirit working in our lives, we have the strength to say no. The faith-walk is a Spirit-walk. "I say then, walk by the Spirit and you will not carry out the desire of the flesh" (Galatians 5:16 HCSB).

Rest in His Spirit. Resist the devastation of sin. There's victory there that never, ever gets old.

Unlike fossilized cat barf. Which incidentally I think I may have identified as throw-up-asaurus retch.

STAYING AWAKE IN HIS WORD

If you think you are standing strong, be careful not to fall. The temptations in your life are no different from what others experience. And God is faithful. He will not allow the temptation to be more than you can stand. When you are tempted, he will show you a way out so that you can endure.

— 1 CORINTHIANS 10:12–13 NLT

This might be the coffee talking, but . . . . . oh wait.
They told me that when the coffee starts talking
I'm supposed to switch to decaf.

Alert to Expecting the Best
— Filled Cup, Chin Up

"Keeping us alert for whatever God will do next. In alert expectancy such as this, we're never left feeling shortchanged"
(ROMANS 5:4–5 *THE MESSAGE*).

COFFEE IS MY favorite food group. It's amazing that my personally overdecorated cup of joe can hit every corner of the food pyramid. I can't help but smile when I've filled my cup, then over-filled it with everything sweet, creamy, flavored, fatty, and wonderful. My cup runneth over.

They make creams now in about every form. Straight, whipped, powdered. Animal, vegetable, mineral. I just love an extra squirt of this flavor, a shot of that one. Of course, every shot adds another 200 calories. With my favorite coffee drink, I can just about reach my entire day's calorie goal even before breakfast.

That's very likely what led to the need for a calorie goal in the first place. I know I've whined about the diet thing already. I think I've figured out some of my diet problems. Just as I'm getting on this new one, wouldn't you know it, I'm now discovering that I'm diet food intolerant. I may change my expectations and instead of buns of steel, settle for buns of cinnamon.

Jiggle Juggle

Expectations can sometimes be heartbreaking. If I'm expecting to wash those cinnamon buns down with my loaded cappuccino, no doubt I'll soon be headed for those dreaded five stages. I've had to deal with them before. The five stages? Denial. Anger. Bargaining. Depression.

Acceptance. Those are the five stages of going up a dress size. And the last one—that "acceptance" thing? It's not a certainty.

I tried on everything in my closet one morning recently. The whole time I was wondering why it was that every goofy thing in there makes me look fat. And then there was the sudden, abysmal realization: It's not the outfit that makes me look fat. It's this *fat* that makes me look fat.

I was just about to head back into another round of those four or five stages when it occurred to me that everything would be much better if I adjusted my attitude. Isn't it rather ironic that I adjust mine with high-calorie coffee?

I was on my second or third cup of attitude adjustment before it started to soak in. You might not guess it, but I actually consider myself a very positive person. Still I have to admit that keeping my chin up is a lot more challenging now that I have more than one. Chin. It seems like keeping my chin up these days is more like . . . well . . . juggling. At the same time, I'm dealing with all the jiggling. And there we go. Right back around for another ride on those stages.

Adjustments on Autofocus

Interestingly, the attitude adjustment and the chin adjustment can be rather connected. Keeping your chin up is not so much about where you keep your chin (or chins, as the case may be). No, it's about where you keep your eyes. When we single-mindedly focus those eyes firmly on Jesus and watch for Him and what He will do, everything changes. Not necessarily our circumstances. But we find our attitude about those circumstances is suddenly on the clearest autoadjust.

It's easy to get stuck in an irksome pattern of focusing on everything negative. There are plenty of frustrations in this life we could dwell on at any one minute. In that same minute, there are a thousand more positives. And even in those frustrations, if we focus on the Lord's ability to work in every situation, they begin to look completely different. Those annoyances become opportunities for the Lord to show Himself strong and mighty to the world.

Paul tells us in Romans 5 to stay alert about expecting the best. I love the way *The Message* paraphrases Romans 5:3–5:

> *There's more to come: We continue to shout our praise even when we're hemmed in with troubles, because we know how troubles can develop passionate patience in us, and how that patience in turn forges the tempered steel of virtue, keeping us alert for whatever God will do next. In alert expectancy such as this, we're never left feeling shortchanged. Quite the contrary—we can't round up enough containers to hold everything God generously pours into our lives through the Holy Spirit!*

Virtue of tempered steel? I'll take that over buns of steel any day. Living our lives expecting the best, understanding the incomparable power our God possesses to work in any and every situation, can take us to a place of perpetually experiencing a faith that never disappoints. As a matter of fact, it takes us to a place of great hope—that unsurpassed hope we read about in chapter 13. Our expectation and our hope are tied tightly together.

A Positive Shout-out

The verse just before the passage in Romans 5 reminds us where the hope is. "We have also obtained access through Him by faith into this grace in which we stand, and we rejoice in the hope of the glory of God" (Romans 5:2 HCSB). The word "rejoice" in this verse is translated from the same word that's paraphrased "shout our praise." It's a word that means to exult without reservation and to find great joy. Positive to the max!

Life filled with expectation is a life filled with hope. It's inexpressibly better than a filled cup. It's a life alert to what God is doing. Focusing on Jesus and everything eternal is focusing on all that is truly unwaveringly positive—everything that really counts. And that leads us to live a life that counts.

"Counts" as in having true significance. Not counting as in calories. Or chins (I call it *chin-ventory*). That's an accounting for another day. Sometimes in five stages.

☙ STAYING AWAKE IN HIS WORD

We know that the One who raised the Lord Jesus will raise us also with Jesus and present us with you. Indeed, everything is for your benefit, so that grace, extended through more and more people, may cause thanksgiving to increase to God's glory. Therefore we do not give up. Even though our outer person is being destroyed, our inner person is being renewed day by day. For our momentary light affliction is producing for us an absolutely incomparable eternal weight of glory. So we do not focus on what is seen, but on what is unseen. For what is seen is temporary, but what is unseen is eternal.

— 2 CORINTHIANS 4:14–18 (HCSB)

Prepared,
Primed

A humongous pot of coffee just crashed through the wall and poured a hot cup for everyone. Your move, giant Kool-Aid pitcher guy.

Alert to Judgment
— Half and Half and Half

> "Make sure you stay alert to these qualities of gentle kindness
> and ruthless severity that exist side by side in God —
> ruthless with the deadwood, gentle with the grafted shoot"
> (Romans 11:21 *The Message*).

GLASS HALF FULL. Glass half empty. Doesn't really matter so much to me. As long as mine is the full half. And also the glass should be a mug. Large. And also it should have coffee in it. And also both halves should be full. And it should all be mine.

I think I like my coffee with half and half. And at least another half. I might also need another side of math.

I saw a bumper sticker recently that said, "I want my coffee and I want it now." I thought, *I want your coffee too. And then after that, I'll want my own coffee.*

Judging from this paragraph, I guess I can be selfish when it comes to coffee.

Judging from This . . .

I was at my favorite coffee café the other day and I overheard a little girl, in the happiest, singsongy little voice saying oh so pleasantly, "Mommy, you've lost lots and lots of weight and you look so pretty." It was one of the sweetest things I've ever heard. Then in her same happy little voice, she chimed, "You're still really fat, though."

Yowch. Pretty harsh, right? Still, cappuccino almost came out my nose. Kids! It's funny that totally innocent honesty can be such a hilarious surprise. There was not even a little hint of animosity or condemnation. You might not believe me, but the whole statement was dripping with love. It was clear to everyone in earshot that this girl loved her mommy—thin or fluffy.

No Half-truths

It's true that humans can be harsh on the judgment side even when we try it in love. But the whole truth is that human beings can miss the mark on righteous judgment as well—soft on sin.

God's love for us is perfect, complete. It's a greater love than we can even comprehend. At the same time, God judges sin and evil. And just as His love is perfect, His judgment is also perfect. Glass half full of judgment? No, God doesn't do things halfway. He hates sin with as much passion as He loves people.

We need to understand that God's judgment is also a part of who our God is. Merciful? Yes. But also holy and just. Sin will never be merely shrugged away. Without His judgment of sin, would He really be holy? Would He really be just?

If God didn't judge sin and evil, just imagine what this world would be like. God is the one who determines right and wrong, so in essence, sin wouldn't even be sin. Evil would be the status quo and heaven would eventually be full of the sin that's gotten our world into the ugly mess it's in. We need a God who judges sin.

We Don't Know the Half of It

Since we're not sinless, God's holiness is a difficult concept for us. It's the shining, brilliant, without-a-speck-of-sin kind of holiness. Sin repels Him. Proverbs 6:16–19 says (HCSB),

> The LORD hates six things; in fact, seven are detestable to Him: arrogant eyes, a lying tongue, hands that shed innocent blood, a heart that plots wicked schemes, feet eager to run to evil, a lying witness who gives false testimony, and one who stirs up trouble among brothers.

Our God also knows everything. He knows sin destroys us. Balanced with His hatred of sin is His great compassion and mercy in sending Christ. "The LORD is gracious and compassionate, slow to anger and rich in love" (Psalm 145:8).

I wonder if we could even truly appreciate His mercy without taking into account His judgment. Paul said in Ephesians 2:4–5 that "because of his great love for us, God, who is rich in mercy, made us alive with Christ even when we were dead in transgressions—it is by grace you have been saved." God's was anything but a half-baked plan. It was a judgment plan and a mercy plan all rolled into one. That one being Jesus Christ.

Nothing Halfhearted

If you have given your life to Christ and trusted in Him to save you, forgive you of your sin, the good news is that Christ took the judgment for your sin upon Himself. Your forgiveness is sure and your eternal blessing with the Lord is a done deal. You've been spared the harsh, righteous judgment of a holy God. If you're not a follower of Christ, you need to know that surrender to Jesus makes the difference between Jesus receiving the judgment of your sin, or you suffering that punishment yourself. "Whoever believes in him is not condemned, but whoever does not believe is condemned already, because he has not believed in the name of the only Son of God" (John 3:18 ESV).

As believers, our response should be to respect God the Judge in every way. And then to appreciate the God of mercy all the more. Contemplating His hatred of sin should remind us to stay on our toes, not letting worldly ideas and philosophies sneak into our thinking and our behavior. God wants our wholehearted devotion. Wholehearted. Never half.

For those of us who aren't as good at math, that might mean three halves.

STAYING AWAKE IN HIS WORD

Therefore, there is now no condemnation for those who are in Christ Jesus, because through Christ Jesus the law of the Spirit who gives life has set you free from the law of sin and death. For what the law was powerless to do because it was weakened by the flesh, God did by sending his own Son in the likeness of sinful flesh to be a sin offering. And so he condemned sin in the flesh, in order that the righteous requirement of the law might be fully met in us, who do not live according to the flesh but according to the Spirit.

— ROMANS 8:1–4

Guy in line taking 20 minutes to order his coffee.
Also mentions he still has no hits at match.com.
Coincidence?

22

Alert to Perseverance
— Is It Live or Is It Mimeograph?

"So we must not get tired of doing good, for we will
reap at the proper time if we don't give up"
(GALATIANS 6:9 HCSB).

EVERYBODY LOOKS FOR the easy button. Sometimes all I want is a
coffee button. Then the other things would be easier anyway.

Since I'm not the best cook on the planet, I'll go ahead and admit
that I would push any and all easy buttons I could get my fingers on to
help things along in the kitchen. I'm definitely a fan, for instance, of all
things frozen. If it can go from freezer to microwave to table, I'm sold.

Grin and Berry It
One night I put together a dinner from everything beautifully frozen.
Strawberry smoothies, a raspberry and blueberry fruit salad, and Salisbury
steak. Strawberry, raspberry, blueberry, and Salisbury. Perfect. An all-fruit
dinner!

And just because the "All Around the Mulberry Bush" song is now
stuck in my head, that doesn't mean I would ever consider frozen weasel.
No matter how much it tastes like chicken. Nope, not even with gravy.

I will say that once we get into all those frozen animal, vegetable, or
mineral meatlike products, Salisbury and otherwise, we're into an area
where I do have some considerable experience. I'll just be honest and tell
you that sometimes it's a good experience. And sometimes it's not. I had
TV dinner chicken the other day that smelled really weird. None for me,
thanks.

Can chicken be mimeographed?

At least I know it couldn't have been spoiled. I think most of the almost meatlike products that I bought at the store this week won't go bad until somewhere around the year 2250. Which, ironically, is about how much some of them cost.

All Around the Salisbury Bush

Looking for convenience? It's not so bad to go frozen. But if you're looking for what's good for you spiritually, it's best to go fire, not frost. Staying hot, really on fire for Christ, may not always be the most convenient, but it's always the best way to live. We weren't meant to waste time running around in circles. We were never called to a mimeograph kind of life either. We're not merely to copy life. We're called to live it! To stay in it! To keep going!

Paul said in 1 Corinthians 9:26–27 (*The Message*),

> *I don't know about you, but I'm running hard for the finish line. I'm giving it everything I've got. No sloppy living for me! I'm staying alert and in top condition. I'm not going to get caught napping, telling everyone else all about it and then missing out myself.*

Sloppy living? None of that for me either, thank you! I want to be one who runs—one who perseveres to the glory of God!

Hurry Up and Wait

Just because you may be waiting, that doesn't mean you're not persevering. Persevering is about continuing in His plan with energy. It's staying focused on who is in control, making sure you know it's God and not you. Proverbs 16:9 (ESV) says, "The heart of man plans his way, but the Lord establishes his steps."

No one likes to wait. I have no doubt that's why microwaves are so popular. Thaw out that dinner in less than ten minutes! But sometimes the Lord lets us wait to remind us who is in control. In every delay—every long line you wait in, every microwave beep you wait on, every traffic light, every class you must finish, every pot that needs to hurry up and boil—you decide if you will let God use the time to grow your faith or if you will fret and stew the time away. Circumstances sometimes cause you to have to wait on someone else to make a decision of some kind and you're essentially "frozen" in place until that person makes a move.

The Lord really can use that frozen place to grow your faith. It's there you learn to rest in His sovereignty and trust His plan. In the big events. And in the trivial, beep-waiting. As we persevere in staying in tune to Him, we see that He has a lesson for us in every wait.

No Weasel Zone

There's no easy button. But perseverance always pays off. We shouldn't try to weasel out of a call to wait. And we should never try to weasel out of a call to go. Become impatient or aggravated, coming or going, and you could miss something wonderful He wants to do in your faith-life. His interest is not so much in your plans or your schedule. It's in developing your character through your patient, determined perseverance.

Perseverance results in blessing. Paul said in Romans 2:7 (AMP), "To those who by patient persistence in well-doing, springing from piety, seek unseen but sure glory and honor and the eternal blessedness of immortality, He will give eternal life."

Peter was all about reminders to keep on persevering in whatever the Lord calls us to.

> *Because the stakes are so high, even though you're up-to-date on all this truth and practice it inside and out, I'm not going to let up for a minute in calling you to attention before it. This is the post to which I've been assigned—keeping you alert with frequent reminders—and I'm sticking to it as long as I live* (2 PETER 1:12–13 *THE MESSAGE*).

Ditto That

I want to stay alert to perseverance too. So I'm dittoing Peter's wake-up reminder. And that, incidentally, has nothing whatsoever to do with mimeographing.

STAYING AWAKE IN HIS WORD

Therefore, since we are surrounded by so great a cloud of witnesses, let us also lay aside every weight, and sin which clings so closely, and let us run with endurance the race that is set before us, looking to Jesus, the founder and perfecter of our faith, who for the joy that was set before him endured the cross, despising the shame, and is seated at the right hand of the throne of God.

— HEBREWS 12:1–2 (ESV)

Coffee is proof that it's morning. Today?
Two cups before it was really true.

Alert to Growing
  — Only My Barista Knows for Sure

> "Enfolded in love, let us grow up in every way and in all things into Him
> Who is the Head, even Christ the Messiah, the Anointed One"
>   (EPHESIANS 4:15 AMP).

I READ THERE are a lot of people who really love their coffee . . . as pest control. No fooling. There are people using coffee to get rid of ants! As if that weren't bizarre enough, I read about folks using coffee grounds as an exfoliator, a plant fertilizer, a furniture stain and a cellulite reducer. The most outlandish coffee use to me was — are you ready for this? — hair color! Wow, now next time I get my hair done, I officially don't know how to answer if they ask me if I'd like coffee.

Coif-ee? I'm not sure who I would ask for that, my hairstylist or my barista.

I guess I should've seen it coming. I give my coffee a lot of attention. I give my hair a lot of attention. Maybe it was inevitable the two should somehow come together.

How Do You Take Your Do?

I'm still having a hard time imagining ordering my hairstyle by the cup. Not to mention, I usually take mine with cream and sugar. Highlights, maybe?

Some people pay close attention to the heat index during the summer. Not me. For me it's all about the "hair" index. Last week the forecast called for several days that were partly frizzy with a chance of a ponytail.

In the winter it's all about the wind chill. Or in hair-weather terms, wind "gel." Too much superhero-strength hair gel in the extreme cold and a lock could snap off. I don't mind attention to hair detail, but snapping to attention doesn't sound healthy in this scenario. I don't like risking my bangs.

Shear Genius

It always bugs me that when I get my hair cut, I only seem to get about a day and a half of good bangs. The length of the bangs changes faster than the weather. It would take a genius to figure out how math and physics works out on this, but it's true that good bangs on Tuesday are bangs that are too long on Wednesday. And those are also the same bangs that will be completely messed up for three weeks because you decided to cut them yourself on Thursday.

Just hope a groundhog doesn't see you. If he sees you've cut them yourself again and you've done another shady job, it's six more weeks of bad bangs. It's painful to just sit at home, waiting for your hair to grow.

Waiting to Grow

Hair lengths will come and go. And come and grow. But on the spiritual side, we need to always be in growth mode. No waiting. Growing in our walk of faith means staying alert to making the Word of God part of each day, staying plugged into a good church, feeding our minds with uplifting music and sermons and staying closely connected with followers who are good examples of godliness. Those things are vital. But listen, you may be doing all of those things and still not growing spiritually. The fact that your knowledge is increasing is good, but it doesn't necessarily mean your faith is increasing or you're growing in the things of God. If you're not growing closer to the Father by allowing His Word to change you and by allowing Him to work through your life, then a major element of spiritual growth is missing.

Spiritual growth is about more than gathering a lot of knowledge about the things of God. It's more than just rituals too. Growth happens as we do what He calls us to do—and it's about becoming more in tune with what His calling is. It happens as we experience true worship. And it happens as we allow Him to work in our lives to the point that we see Him using us to help someone else grow as well.

I love how He so often grows us so that we can touch the life of another. You'll know you're maturing in the faith when you see the truth you receive from God fleshed out in your life in how you follow Him, how you love Him, how you serve Him, and how you share Him. Your life with Him should be warm and personal and that should show up in everything you do.

Crowning Glory

Paul said, "God wants the combination of his steady, constant calling and warm, personal counsel in Scripture to come to characterize us, keeping us alert for whatever he will do next. May our dependably steady and warmly personal God develop maturity in you so that you get along with each other as well as Jesus gets along with us all," (Romans 15:4–5 *The Message*).

Your salvation came power-packed with purpose. You're growing as you embrace that purpose, walking in faith as you glorify His name by loving Him and loving others. There are hurting people in this world who desperately need to see your faith-walk, to understand the glory of His name, and to experience the love of the Father.

The growth that you long to see happen in your life? Your heavenly Father wants it too. That's where the power comes in. Paul said in Philippians 1:6 (AMP),

And I am convinced and sure of this very thing, that He Who began a good work in you will continue until the day of Jesus Christ, right up to the time of His return, developing that good work and perfecting and bringing it to full completion in you.

All He needs is your willingness and He will keep up the sanctifying work that began at your salvation. He can use you to show His glory and to touch the lives of others with that glory.

Enthusiastic Attention

Coffee gets my attention. Hair gets my attention. Staying alert to my spiritual growth? That gets my attention on an entirely different level. Attention to the max. Not just looking like a spiritual person, but energetically putting heart and soul into letting my relationship with the God of the universe change my world. Paul charged us to "never be lazy, but work hard and serve the Lord enthusiastically" (Romans 12:11 NLT).

That inspires me, motivates me, energizes me — gets me oh so very excited!

And I'll bet I know what you're thinking but, no, for my next hair color I'm not necessarily planning to go decaf.

STAYING AWAKE IN HIS WORD

For this reason I remind you to fan into flame the gift of God, which is in you through the laying on of my hands. For God did not give us a spirit of timidity, but a spirit of power, of love and of self-discipline. So do not be ashamed to testify about our Lord, or ashamed of me his prisoner. But join with me in suffering for the gospel, by the power of God, who has saved us and called us to a holy life — not because of anything we have done but because of his own purpose and grace. This grace was given us in Christ Jesus before the beginning of time, but it has now been revealed through the appearing of our Savior, Christ Jesus, who has destroyed death and has brought life and immortality to light through the gospel.

— 2 Timothy 1:6–10

Remember when you could order coffee in four syllables or less? Now it takes me at least a dozen. At about $1.50 every couple of syllables.

*Alert to Staying Faithful in Hard Times
— Fall Up, Not Apart*

> "It is by faith you stand firm"
> (2 CORINTHIANS 1:24).

MY HUSBAND IS a dunker. I confess, I'm still a little appalled by this. I'm not sure he'll ever have a cup of coffee and a doughnut at the same time where the doughnut stays dry. Toast, cinnamon rolls, biscuits, toaster pastries, cookies—they're not safe either. Hamhock? I wouldn't count it out.

Me? I would never dunk. It's mostly because I truly can't stand the thought of "coffee gumbo." You totally lose me when you get to that last sip and you don't know whether to chew, try to strain, or just swallow.

I still haven't figured out what a person is supposed to do when the doughnut gets oversaturated and a hunk of it goes in. I'm afraid that in my mind, my morning would fall apart the same time as the doughnut.

Fallout

Ever have one of those days when it seems like too many of the little things sort of fall apart? The other day I dropped my purse and half the contents fell out. As I was trying to gather it all up, I dropped my phone and the battery fell out. A little later I opened the fridge door and the butter fell out. By that time . . . I was totally afraid to do my hair.

Fallout? It can be scary. That's before you even consider anything radioactive.

Sometimes it's not just the little things that fall apart. We live in a fallen world. That means that now and again we'll fall on hard times.

Maybe we fall short of a vital goal, have a falling out with a trusted friend, fall ill, or become the fall guy for some evil person's scheme. So many ways to fall! Ever so often, does life feel a little like you used the blender without the lid? Everything inside falls out. Well, actually it's more like "falling up," but still.

Falling Up

Whatever may *befall* us, we can trust our heavenly Father in every single circumstance. Trust means letting go. It's knowing that He is there and that He is enough. This is the "trust fall" that will make the difference between joyfully walking in faith or falling between the cracks—getting stuck in darkness, depression, and defeat. Don't fall away. Fall back—do a trust fall softly and safely into the arms of Jesus. He is trustworthy. He will catch you. And He can keep your life moving in the right direction. It really is falling *up*!

When we let difficult circumstances cause us to fall out of step with Jesus, we're neglecting the one thing in life that gives us real purpose and sustaining joy. That's just asking for a fall into a dark place of hopelessness. There life is its most dismal. We've talked about your enemy, who sees this fallen world as his turf. He will lie to you to keep your thoughts and desires mired in the here and now instead of focusing them heavenward. He'll tell you up is down and down is up, crushing your hopes all the while. Don't *fall* for his lies!

You have choices to make every day. You choose whether you will trust God and rest in Him and His faithful goodness in every circumstance, or if you will focus on your problems rather than your Problem Fixer. Your choice determines your perspective, your fruitfulness, your joy factor—your quality of life.

Whate'er Befalls

Difficulties are anything but fun. We mentioned Romans 5 in chapter 20. Take another look at Paul's instructions to "glory in our sufferings." Why? "Because we know that suffering produces perseverance; perseverance, character; and character, hope" (Romans 5:3–4). Suffering is pressure. The pressure of our difficulties can become like the skillful potter's pressure on pliable clay as he shapes the clay into something extraordinary. God can use suffering to mold us if we will trust more and squirm less. The word *perseverance* in Romans 5:4 is a word that literally means "to remain under." A little patience on the Potter's wheel leads to stronger character and a hope that never disappoints.

Often our trials will chip away at some sneaky pride in our lives. And pride goes before . . . a what? "Pride goes before destruction, a haughty spirit before a fall" (Proverbs 16:18). There are times when a life-shaping trial is a loving deterrent to a life-damaging fall.

There's also a testimony to this world every time we stay patient on the wheel, alert to what the Lord is doing, remaining faithful no matter the difficulties. Paul said in 2 Corinthians 6:4 (*The Message*), "People are watching us as we stay at our post, alertly, unswervingly . . . in hard times, tough times, bad times."

Falling Face First

God's Word tells us not to let tough times catch us off-guard.

> *Dear friends, do not be surprised at the painful trial you are suffering, as though something strange were happening to you. But rejoice that you participate in the sufferings of Christ, so that you may be overjoyed when his glory is revealed. . . . So then, those who suffer according to God's will should commit themselves to their faithful Creator and continue to do good* (1 PETER 4:12–13, 19).

Painful situations are part of this life. But we're instructed to keep on doing good.

We can do that by the strength He gives. Where do we fall? On our faces before Him. First. Pray your way through the trial. He will respond and He will lead you through—whate'er befalls you. Fanny Crosby wrote the lyrics to the hymn, "All the Way My Savior Leads Me." In the hymn she touches on trials—and being born blind in the 1800s she certainly had her share. She writes:

All the way my Savior leads me;
What have I to ask beside?
· *Can I doubt His tender mercy,*
Who thro' life has been my guide?
Heav'nly peace, divinest comfort,
Here by faith in Him to dwell!
For I know, whate'er befall me,
Jesus doeth all things well;
For I know, whate'er befall me,
Jesus doeth all things well.

Whatever befalls us, He will lead—with tender mercy, heavenly peace, divine comfort.

Not as Easy as Falling Off a Log

As for my morning full of fallout the other day? It hasn't been easy. After the purse, the phone, and the butter, gotta tell you, I had no small amount of anxiety when it came time to brush my teeth. Not to mention, now it seems no one wants me to hold their babies.

STAYING AWAKE IN HIS WORD

Consider it a sheer gift, friends, when tests and challenges come at you from all sides. You know that under pressure, your faith-life is forced into the open and shows its true colors. So don't try to get out of anything prematurely. Let it do its work so you become mature and well-developed, not deficient in any way.

— JAMES 1:2–4 (*THE MESSAGE*)

I step my most gracefully when I'm carrying my coffee cup from the pot to the table and I filled it too full. It's almost like ballet, except that I look very afraid.

Alert to Thankfulness
— Thanks a Latte

"Stay alert, with your eyes wide open in gratitude"
(COLOSSIANS 4:2 *THE MESSAGE*).

FOR FAR TOO many years I lived as one of the "unenlightened." Meaning I didn't like coffee. At all. But I always loved the smell. I can't even count the number of times I would get a nose-full, and I'd think I just had to try it again. One sip and I'd pull a major face. Then I would put it away for another few years. I always thought it would be so great if coffee tasted like it smelled.

You're going to think I'm making this up, but one morning I woke up and wanted to smell it. So I made a pot. I made it exclusively for my nose's sake. But then after sniffing—even though my past experience told me not to do it—I poured myself a cup, sugar-and-creamed it up as I had done so many times before and . . . I tasted. Lo and behold, there it was! I tasted the smell.

Since then I've tried and loved most every coffee, cappuccino, espresso, and latte in the book. I'm not sure what kept my nose and taste buds from communicating all those years, but I'm so thankful they finally got it together. Tasting and inhaling are a couple of my favorite things.

A Breath of Fresh Air
Wearing my "breathing optional" jeans is another one of those things that causes me to appreciate inhaling. Actually, it's taking them off that's a real breath of fresh air.

When my children were younger, I remember wearing a pair of the death jeans and having to instruct the kids with something like, "OK, now if Mommy passes out, never mind the CPR. *Unbutton the jeans,* thank you."

Thanks-prompting is such an essential part of life. Raising five kids, I wonder how many times over the years I said the words, "What do you say?" I always asked the question in the textbook mother-lilt. My kids are in their teens and 20s now. If you're still in the prompting years, you're probably wondering if you'll have to thank-coach forever. This isn't the answer you're wanting, but yes. Yes, you will. Just for fun I asked one of my 20somethings the other day, "What's the magic word?" Know what the answer was? "Abracadabra." I so should've prompted more often.

What Do You Say?

Ever find your personal worship time feeling a little trivial—not as joy-filled—but you can't quite put your finger on why? Maybe a thanks prompt is in order there too. Thanks is an essential part of a healthy faith-life. Sometimes in periods of listlessness we discover that we've neglected this important part of entering into worship. In Psalm 100:4, the psalmist gives us some "keys to the gates" of worship, as it were. We're told to enter His gates with thanksgiving. The gates of the temple represented God's most holy presence. The people were to enter into the presence of their holy God through those gates "with thanksgiving." Again, Psalm 95:2 (ESV) says, "Let us come into his presence with thanksgiving."

Thanks and praise are a little like an "abracadabra, open sesame." Thanksgiving is the threshold to a deeper, more genuine worship. As we give thanks to God, we remember His faithfulness, His love and mercy, His blessing—His glorious provision. Through gratitude, we find our focus changing from the things we think we need or the things we would like God to do for us, to a meeker place of delighting in what He's already done. We begin to recognize anew areas where He's already so graciously at work. We're moved to love and adore Him all the more. Extraordinary things happen in the presence of God through our thanksgiving.

The psalmist said in Psalm 107:21–22 (NLT) says,

Let them praise the Lord for his great love and for the wonderful things he has done for them. Let them offer sacrifices of thanksgiving and sing joyfully about his glorious acts.

Our thanksgiving is a sacrifice to Him. It's our offering. God tells us in Psalm 50:23 (CEV), "The sacrifice that honors me is a thankful heart."

A Whole New Appreciation

It's time to take on a new appreciation of appreciation. Drinking it in. Making it part of our thinking. Making it part of every breath as we walk out our day. We can become alert to thankfulness as we:

- EXPERIENCE APPRECIATION — Take the time to recognize all that God has done. So many things miss our notice if we're not cued in to experiencing true gratitude.
- EXPRESS APPRECIATION — It's not enough simply to recognize that we're blessed, we need thank our gracious God for those blessings.
- EXHIBIT APPRECIATION — True thankfulness will show up in our attitudes and actions. It changes the way we respond to our Father and how we respond to those around us.

Offer thanks in every way. Add it to your everyday coming and going. Express it as regularly and freely as you breathe in and out. Notice — breathe in — His goodness. Exhale gratitude and worship. You could very well find yourself ushered through the gates of His presence like never before. How glorious it is when our worship takes us deeper through thanksgiving. Drink in His greatness and let it become praise you offer right back to Him. "Oh, taste and see that the LORD is good!" (Psalm 34:8 ESV).

On Tasting and Seeing

Incidentally, I'm also thankful I retasted the coffee. Of course, a few too many lattes and I have another ugly jeans situation. I would sigh heavily about it, but I might accidentally launch a button.

STAYING AWAKE IN HIS WORD

Let us enter His presence with thanksgiving; let us shout triumphantly to Him in song. For the LORD is a great God, a great King above all gods. The depths of earth are in His hand, and the mountain peaks are His. The sea is His; He made it. His hands formed the dry land. Come, let us worship and bow down; let us kneel before the LORD our Maker. For He is our God, and we are the people of His pasture, the sheep under His care.

— PSALM 95:2–7 (HCSB)

Coffee. Part of this nutritious breakfast.
And lunch. And dinner.

Alert to Building Good Character — We Don't Know Beans

> "So don't lose a minute in building on what you've been given,
> complementing your basic faith with good character"
> (2 Peter 1:5 *The Message*).

SOME PEOPLE TELL me coffee upsets their stomach. How sad. I hope that never happens to me. Because I'd hate to give it up. You know. Give up feeling good.

If it's some sort of gastric distress—and since coffee is made from the coffee bean—why doesn't someone come up with "Coffee-Bean-o"? Just a suggestion.

In gastric distresses of different import, I had an interesting conversation with a couple of my kids a few months ago. My son Jordan was making a passionate argument about something or another and he ended his proclamation with "Mom. Seriously." Only I can't express it with the same punch he did because he totally power-burped the last word.

My daughter Kaley said, "Yeah, Jordan. It always helps your argument when you belch it."

Jordan responded with: "Yeah, that's why they do it all the time on the Senate floor."

You Hardly Ever Hear This in the Senate

OK, I'm sorry, but it cracked me up when I got this visual of all our statesmen in a "who can burp their point the loudest" competition. I have to wonder if this could end a few of those disputes on Capitol Hill. Or maybe start some new ones.

Alert to Building Good Character—We Don't Know Beans • 151

Anyway, no one really asks why neither I nor any of my children have ever run for public office. And while I'll probably never represent any of my fellow Americans in Congress, I do need to keep in mind that I'm always representing Christ.

The Amplified Version of 2 Corinthians 5:20 tells us that "we are Christ's ambassadors, God making His appeal as it were through us. We, as Christ's personal representatives, beg you for His sake to lay hold of the divine favor now offered you and be reconciled to God."

A representative? As a matter of fact, I've already been elected. You have, too, if you've given your life to Christ. What an honor it is to represent Him! I pray regularly that the Lord will help me communicate His truth in whatever way He wants me to communicate it. May it happen through each of us as His representatives. However He wants us to communicate it and to every person He wants us to communicate it to. Seriously.

Chain Letter

In Paul's letter to the Ephesians he referred to himself as an ambassador as well.

> *Pray also for me, that whenever I speak, words may be given me so that I will fearlessly make known the mystery of the gospel, for which I am an ambassador in chains. Pray that I may declare it fearlessly, as I should"* (EPHESIANS 6:19–20).

There is usually prestige connected to becoming an ambassador or a representative. But an "ambassador in chains"? It may be tougher to find people to run for that office or make themselves available for that appointment.

But when we're looking at the appointment from an eternal perspective, it's startling what an honor we find it is to be called to passionately lobby those who don't know Jesus. We are to "beg" them, as the passage in 2 Corinthians describes it, to be reconciled to God through Christ.

Our office is an honor, yes, but it also holds a calling to good character. Not exactly like some politicians do character. But like they should. Only in a much more vital, urgent work. As representatives, we're called to model good character. As followers of Christ, we're called to be alert to good character to please the One we follow. Righteous living should be the goal of our faith walk.

Willing to Spill the Beans

So how do we work to build good character? Not by hiding our failures. Not by pretending we're perfect. Probably not several of the other ways people generally assume either. Part of developing good character is being able to be transparent. Often we're too embarrassed to admit our failings. When Christ comes into our lives, our sin is forgiven and we're righteous because of His sin payment. We begin a sanctification process that takes us in the direction of holier living, that's true. Yet our struggle with our sin nature continues for the rest of our journey on this planet.

Pretending to be perfect and trying to arrive at that perfection on our own can actually steer us away from the good character we desire and the righteous walk of faith we're seeking. We can't rely on our own abilities for character building any more than we could rely on ourselves to take care of our sin. We need Christ.

During Jesus' ministry, He chose to hang around those with the worst reputations. Probably not a great political move if Jesus was running for office. But in His words, He came to "seek and to save the lost" (Luke 19:10 ESV). When the Pharisees asked the disciples why Jesus was lowering Himself to eat with low-life sinners and tax collectors, Jesus told them, "Those who are well don't need a doctor, but the sick do need one. I didn't come to call the righteous, but sinners" (Mark 2:17 HCSB). *The New Living Translation* phrases it this way: "Healthy people don't need a doctor—sick people do. I have come to call not those who think they are righteous, but those who know they are sinners."

Jesus came to heal the spiritually sick at the point they recognized their inability to heal themselves. When we wake up to our own inadequacy, we can then fully realize our desperate need for Him. While most people view success as having authority, control, and power within, Jesus wants people to realize their brokenness. It's then that He can work. And this is the foundation for the righteous walk of faith. It's where good character is built.

Self-Effort? Not Worth Beans

Your own accomplishments won't amount to a hill of beans apart from Christ. Realize your weakness and your neediness and follow passionately after the Savior. When you do, good character begins to develop right before your eyes—sometimes without you even realizing it. Following passionately after the Savior sparks a hunger for His Word, a heart for service, a call to prayer—all those things that will build godliness and good character all the more.

Believe it or not, that's also very often a topic of conversation between me and my kids. Even though we're not members of the House of Representatives, we're ever seeking to challenge each other to remember that we do have a house full of representatives. And the character of Christ should be well represented in each of us.

Back on the political side though, can you imagine some of our conversations near any election time? Something like, "I'd never vote for that guy. Why, he probably couldn't burp his way out of a paper bag."

STAYING AWAKE IN HIS WORD

So don't lose a minute in building on what you've been given, complementing your basic faith with good character, spiritual understanding, alert discipline, passionate patience, reverent wonder, warm friendliness, and generous love, each dimension fitting into and developing the others.

— 2 PETER 1:5–7 (*THE MESSAGE*)

I gave up coffee one time.
One of the worst half hours of my life.

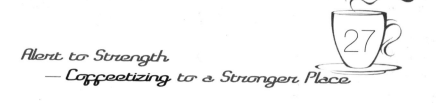

"Be alert and on your guard;
stand firm in your faith . . . grow in strength!"
(1 CORINTHIANS 16:13 AMP).

MOST DAYS I feel a deep need to *coffeetize* myself to a better, more caffeinated place. Not that it's a spiritual or celestial experience really, but I do think it does have some *Star Trek*-ian qualities. Boldly going, and all. And if I ever have to go instant, for instance, I've decided to forget the Folger's crystals. From here on out, I'm going with something closer to dylithium crystals. "Bean" me up, coffee.

I guess if I'm going to keep my head in the coffee stars, seems the least I can do is make a note of the weather up here. Today's coffee forecast: dark with a 50 percent chance of hazelnut. Look for scattered creamer in the afternoon.

Some mornings I feel like I need a downpour before I can get the neurons sufficiently firing on at least most cylinders. One of my finer qualities? Probably not, no.

However, not to toot my own horn or anything, but I think I do have some very unique and useful character qualities. Granted, most better psychoanalysts might not refer to them as "character qualities" as much as "symptoms," but still.

Qualities Versus Symptoms
I think writers acquire an exclusive symptom or two . . . make that a "quality" or two . . . that others don't necessarily encounter. Maybe it's the

inordinate amount of rejection we're called to deal with, but insecurity is so often the order of the day. Not to mention that when fiction writers hear new little voices in their heads, they never medicate. No, they actually encourage the little voices. And then publish them.

This week, though, I experienced a "quality" beyond voices. It's a weird thing that happens to me now and again. I look over the writing *du jour* and I keep thinking I've misspelled words—even when I haven't.

I think I might be a *typo-chondriac*.

Interestingly enough, if the psycho-professionals come up with a 12-step program for *typo-chondriacs*, I'm pretty sure step one will be admitting you *don't* have a problem.

Where Do We Find Spiritual Muscle?

When it comes to successfully walking out this life of faith in Christ, though, we have to recognize right from the get-go our complete lack of ability to make it happen ourselves. We do have a problem. And without surrendering to the leadership of God's Holy Spirit, there's no hope for resolving that problem. No 12-step program. No self-help book. Personally speaking, I don't even have a horn to toot. Not a leg to stand on. Not a keyboard to type on. It's got to be all Him and zero me.

You'd think that would cause a more intense insecurity than even a writer has to bear. But it doesn't. As a matter of fact, it's the exact opposite. There is great security in knowing that I don't have to depend on my own abilities. There is even greater security in knowing that I can so completely depend on the One who is all-powerful. Paul reminds us in Philippians 3:3 (NLT) that "we rely on what Christ Jesus has done for us. We put no confidence in human effort."

We Got Nuttin'

The *Amplified Version* of Philippians 3:3 puts it this way: "Put no confidence or dependence on what we are in the flesh and on outward privileges and physical advantages and external appearances." That pretty much settles it. Nothing we've done. Nothing we've said. Nothing we are. Nothing inside us. Nothing outside us. Victory in the walk of faith will only happen as we rely totally and completely on the all-powerful one. And in Him our security is sure.

So it's not such a terrible thing to recognize that even though I'm a writer, with all the built-in insecurities and various "qualities" that come with it, I don't have to live in insecurity. There's freedom in recognizing I have nothing to offer in and of myself, but that "I can do all things through Christ who strengthens me" (Philippians 4:13 NKJV).

Whatever our qualities or symptoms, we're called to stay alert to becoming strong and to becoming strong the right way. We are to *coffeetize* ourselves to an exclusively Jesus place. Jesus Himself told us in Luke 21:36 (NLT), "Keep alert at all times. And pray that you might be strong." And Paul doesn't mince words in Ephesians 6:10 when he tells us to "be strong in the Lord and in his mighty power." We never have to worry about a lack of strength when we're depending on His. We are strong through His strength—His mighty power.

In Other Symptoms . . .
That's especially refreshing to dwell on when I realize that on top of my *typo-chondria*, I think I might be coming down with a touch of kleptomania.

Gee, I hope there's something I can take for that.

STAYING AWAKE IN HIS WORD

In conclusion, be strong in the Lord, be empowered through your union with Him; draw your strength from Him, that strength which His boundless might provides. Put on God's whole armor, the armor of a heavy-armed soldier which God supplies, that you may be able successfully to stand up against all the strategies and the deceits of the devil.

— Ephesians 6:10–11 (AMP)

I found biblical grounds that my husband should make the coffee. "He-brews." A whole book. That's solid biblical "grounds," right?

Alert to Keeping the Faith
— Steady as She Grows

"It is by faith you stand firm"

(2 CORINTHIANS 1:24).

I JUST FINISHED my morning run. Wait. Did I say morning run? I meant morning doughnut.

Most of the time if you hear me mention my "morning run," it refers to my trip to Starbucks. And it's in a car. Maybe even in my ducky pajama pants.

I was considering actually going for a real jog this morning though. Really I was. Then I decided to just do a Google Earth search of a nice, scenic route in my neighborhood and then trace it with my eyes several times. My eyeballs are in the shape of their lives.

Firming Up

While some call my morning doughnut your basic overload of dough, fat, and every form of sugar, I prefer to think of it as carb-loading. I do admit that I've been carb-loading since around 1985. OK, yes, that's a lot of carbs. But on the upside, I'm one of the few people truly carbohydrate-prepared for a spur of the moment 500K.

If only I could run a race using just my eyes and all these carbs. Unfortunately my thighs might have to come along too. I try not to mention running where my thighs can hear me. They get upset and start to spark. The thighs tell me the spark is all about friction, but I think that's probably just the way thighs exhibit a panic attack.

Alert and Race-Ready

I can put off my thigh-readiness for the time being, but my soul? Never. Soul-readiness is essential for running this life-race with alertness and running it in victory. Firm thighs would be nice, but a firm faith is critical. We're instructed to pay attention to our faith. "Keep alert. Be firm in your faith" (1 Corinthians 16:13 CEV).

God is calling us to attention. He's calling us to stay alert to our faith condition. A firm faith is a steady faith. It's one that's unshakable. Resolute. Unwavering. So how can we make sure we're alert to keeping our faith in shape? We can start by hanging on to these keeping the faith "keepers."

- KEEP YOUR FINGER IN HIS WORD. You'll find yourself stronger in your faith as you learn more about the Father, His will, His ways, and His trustworthiness. And we're building faith muscle every time we make a decision according to the wisdom we find in the Bible. "Your statutes are my delight; they are my counselors" (Psalm 119:24).

- KEEP ON SEEKING HIM IN PRAYER, asking Him to enable you to keep the faith and continually asking Him to supply everything you need for living well. How He loves to answer! Jesus said, "And whatever you ask for in prayer, having faith and really believing, you will receive" (Matthew 21:22 AMP).

- KEEP HOLDING ONTO THE CERTAINTY THAT THE FATHER HAS A PLAN FOR YOU—a good one. "For I know the plans I have for you, says the Lord. They are plans for good and not for disaster, to give you a future and a hope" (Jeremiah 29:11 NLT). Set aside your own plan. Exchange it for His grand one. You can trust Him. The Lord says in Psalm 32:8 (NLT), "I will guide you along the best pathway for your life. I will advise you and watch over you."

- KEEP YOUR HEAD. Understand that God is in control and, again, that you can fully trust Him every moment of every day in every circumstance. The psalmist reminds us Psalm 103:19 (CEV) that He "rules the whole creation." He is all-powerful—nothing you encounter is too much for Him to handle.

- KEEP ON OBEYING HIM WITH EVERYTHING YOU'VE GOT, fully surrendering to Him in loving submission. "In fact, this is love for God: to keep his commands. And his commands are not burdensome" (1 John 5:3).
- KEEP THE FIRE BURNING. If you sense your excitement in the things of the Lord fading, fan the flames by refocusing your attention on Him. Sometimes it's good to spark. See if there's any sin that has crept in and get rid of it. Then depend on the Holy Spirit to keep you fessed up and growing. He is faithful to rekindle your heart. Pay attention to His promptings.
- KEEP ON LOVING OTHERS WITH THE LOVE THAT HE GIVES YOU. Keeping the faith means getting involved in the lives of others in His name. Paul and those with him mentioned their thanks to God for the Christians in Colossae because, he said, "we have heard of your faith in Christ Jesus and of the love you have for all God's people" (Colossians 1:4). A shipshape faith shows up in how we love.

Keep On Keeping On

Keeping the faith means not giving up, not giving in, never quitting! Just the opposite. The evidence of a "faith kept" is growth. A firm faith flourishes. Paul talks about that stop-being-a-baby kind of growth in Ephesians 4:14–16:

> *Then we will no longer be infants, tossed back and forth by the waves, and blown here and there by every wind of teaching and by the cunning and craftiness of people in their deceitful scheming. Instead, speaking the truth in love, we will grow to become in every respect the mature body of him who is the head, that is, Christ. From him the whole body, joined and held together by every supporting ligament, grows and builds itself up in love, as each part does its work.*

Babies quit. Baby believers are wishy-washy in what they believe and how they respond. We're to be growing in faith and growing in every spiritual discipline, becoming mature as we keep Christ as our head. He's the one who makes the whole body — all believers — work together and develop godly maturity. I love it that He grows each of us individually at the same time He's growing us as a body, readying us all the more for the faith race. Out of the spiritual diapers and into the running shoes!

Firm Decision

So whatever my thighs decide to do, the rest of me has no choice but to grow. To firm up. To make a resolute, firm decision to give my faith-life my focused attention. We see from 2 Corinthians 1:24 at the first of this chapter that "it is by faith you stand firm."

And just so you won't think that I've replaced every one of my brain cells with doughnut batter, yes I do know that being soul-ready and body-firm are not mutually exclusive. I wouldn't exactly call it a "firm decision," but I'm gradually working up to a regular fitness routine. Very, very gradually. I'll probably start with a rigorous eye-tracing of a half-marathon.

Impressed?

STAYING AWAKE IN HIS WORD

Be alert and on your guard; stand firm in your faith, your conviction respecting man's relationship to God and divine things, keeping the trust and holy fervor born of faith and a part of it. Act like men and be courageous; grow in strength!

— 1 Corinthians 16:13 (AMP)

Hey, did I ever tell you about the time the coffee pot didn't shut off? It stayed on all day. By evening, voila! Coffee jerky.

29

Alert to Discipline
— Hot and Cold Running Faith

"Mark a life of discipline and live wisely; don't squander
your precious life. Blessed the man, blessed the woman,
who listens to me, awake and ready for me each morning"
(PROVERBS 8:33–34 *THE MESSAGE*).

THERE'S NOTHING LIKE a hot cup of coffee. So forgive me if I'm a little whiny here, but it seems like the time segment in which coffee is at its absolute perfect temperature is only about three seconds long.

You pour the coffee. It's too hot. So you figure you'll wait three minutes for it to cool. But somewhere during minute two, you start reading an article. You look up at the end of the article and you're already six minutes too late. Cold coffee. So you stick it in the microwave. But then it's too hot. So you figure you'll wait three minutes for it to cool. But somewhere during minute two, the phone rings. Sigh.

Since I'm already whining and sighing, I might as well tell you that it's even worse at a restaurant. The waitress will come by to give you a "warm up" — which translates to not enough hot coffee to warm up what's in your cup but enough to totally mess with your cream-to-sugar-to-coffee ratio. The only thing that helps me not whine about the cold coffee is the fudge cake.

It's Tough Not to Fudge

I'm trying to eat better. Really I am. But I was at a buffet this past week and as I was heading toward the salad bar, I'm just sure I heard the fudge cake calling my name. I tried to ignore it, but it's downright impressive how persistent an exceptionally good-looking fudge cake can be. "Get thee behind me, fudge cake!" I yelled. At that point, I'm pretty sure I saw the fudge cake smile. I looked toward the salad bar for some sort of hope. Then back at the fudge cake—which, incidentally, was still calling my name. The salad bar? It fell strangely silent.

Discipline can be so tough in every area of life. As far as spiritual discipline goes, we're called to stay alert and stay in training. Paul coached Timothy, and us, too, in 1 Timothy 4:7 (AMP): "Train yourself toward godliness (piety), keeping yourself spiritually fit." Less spiritual fudge cake. More spiritual trips to the gym.

Heading to the Gym

At least we can know we're in good company in the struggle. The very same Paul who said we should train and keep spiritually fit also said,

> *For I do not understand my own actions. For I do not do what I want, but I do the very thing I hate. For I know that nothing good dwells in me, that is, in my flesh. For I have the desire to do what is right, but not the ability to carry it out. For I do not do the good I want, but the evil I do not want is what I keep on doing. For I delight in the law of God, in my inner being, but I see in my members another law waging war against the law of my mind and making me captive to the law of sin that dwells in my members* (Romans 7:15, 18–19, 22–23 ESV).

Discipline is tied into that battle to obey. "Discipline" is following Christ as His "disciple." Are you frustrated in your walk of faith? Check the discipline factor. If we want a life filled with victory, purpose, and fruit, then we simply have to build discipline. Proverbs 10:17 (*The Message*) says that "the road to life is a disciplined life."

I feel Paul's frustration in the next verse in that Romans passage. "Wretched man that I am! Who will deliver me from this body of death?" (Romans 7:24 ESV). Paul wanted to do the right thing. And yet often didn't. I can so relate!

So how did Paul handle living in a body of flesh—one that fights to have its own way? Verse 25 is a wonderful relief, "Thanks be to God through Jesus Christ our Lord!" Who will deliver this body? Jesus! He delivered us ultimately at His sacrificial death on the Cross. And He will be our strength at every point we will surrender in trust and obedience.

Grace-ipline

A well-adjusted life balances discipline with grace. There will be times when we fail. The flesh can be more persistent and seductive than the fudgiest fudge cake. Without excusing our sin, we need to still understand that there is grace for every failure. And we need to be assured that God is yet at work. I love *The Message*'s paraphrase of Ephesians 3:20: "God can do anything, you know—far more than you could ever imagine or guess or request in your wildest dreams! He does it not by pushing us around but by working within us, his Spirit deeply and gently within us."

It's not His bullying. It's our invitation. As we invite Him in to work in us and strengthen us, He begins that strengthening from the inside-out. "Not a brute strength," as Paul says a few verses earlier, "but a glorious inner strength—that Christ will live in you as you open the door and invite him in" (Ephesians 3:16–17 *The Message*).

Discipline is not about whipping ourselves into shape. Real strength comes as we understand our weaknesses, just as Paul did. In 2 Corinthians 12:9 the Lord said to him, "My grace is sufficient for you, for my power is made perfect in weakness." Want to let the Lord show off His power? Give Him your every weakness. Watch what He will do! Isaiah 40:29 says that He "gives strength to the weary and increases the power of the weak." Just think. There's a powerful happening packed deep inside your every weakness. Each one can show off the power of your amazing God!

An All-You-Can-Need Buffet

So what do we do? We surrender to the Father, trust in His strength, and do whatever it takes to keep running the race. Keep running!

Paul tells us in Philippians 2:13 (AMP) that the Father works in us giving us the desire to obey, then He gives us the power to make it happen. "Not in your own strength for it is God Who is all the while effectually at work in you energizing and creating in you the power and desire, both to will and to work for His good pleasure and satisfaction and delight." He gives you absolutely everything you need—almost buffet style. And working for His good pleasure, satisfaction, and delight? There's no sweeter work. I'm telling you, fudge cake can't even compare.

Incidentally, I never whine about fudge cake. It's always the right temperature. There's probably a lesson in there somewhere. Because of that I've now determined that fudge cake is also educational. If I keep this thought thread unraveling long enough, I might eventually conclude it's tax deductible.

STAYING AWAKE IN HIS WORD

But what happens when we live God's way? He brings gifts into our lives, much the same way that fruit appears in an orchard — things like affection for others, exuberance about life, serenity. We develop a willingness to stick with things, a sense of compassion in the heart, and a conviction that a basic holiness permeates things and people. We find ourselves involved in loyal commitments, not needing to force our way in life, able to marshal and direct our energies wisely.

— GALATIANS 5:22–23 (*THE MESSAGE*)

Has anyone seen my inspiration lying around here anywhere? Oh, wait. There it is. It was right there at the bottom of my coffee cup the whole time.

Alert to God's Ways
— Cafe Before Beauty?

> "God made my life complete when I placed all
> the pieces before him. Now I'm alert to God's ways"
> (PSALM 18:20, 22 *THE MESSAGE*).

I INADVERTENTLY CAUGHT a glimpse of myself in the mirror one morning precaffeine. I try not to let that happen. But this particular morning I flicked on the light and was startled to attention by that first half-glance in the mirror. That person was so not me.

First of all, I'm much thinner. The chick in the mirror? A few too many creams in her coffee, I'd say. Secondly, her fashion sense was either behind mine or way too ahead of it. That hair? I'm pretty sure I've seen that same do in anime (Japanese cartoons). Way too Bride of Frankenstein for me.

She also had more wrinkles than I do, though I'd never be so tacky as to point that out. It didn't help in the least that she had some major pillow marks. It looked like she'd caught a few z's . . . to the face.

How many cups of coffee does it take to fill in pillow marks that are bigger than the pillow? Either way, no doubt those ruts would be there past noon. That just didn't seem right—and I may never sleep again. I should never have turned on that light.

Something to Reflect On

No worries. Not really. We have something so much better to reflect on. As those who follow the God of the universe, we're called to be "reflections" of His glory. I need to make sure I'm concerned about what kind of spiritual image I'm reflecting so much more than I fret over that precoffee image of me.

As we contemplate reflecting His glory, we become more and more alert to His ways—we become more like Him. And every time we see something in the mirror that just doesn't seem right, it's our glorious Lord who will take care of any transforming that's needed, all by the power of His Holy Spirit working inside us. "We all, with unveiled faces, are looking as in a mirror at the glory of the Lord and are being transformed into the same image from glory to glory; this is from the Lord who is the Spirit" (2 Corinthians 3:18 HCSB).

So as we become alert to His ways, how are our decisions affected? Sometimes it may seem like a bit of a shot in the dark. But it's always our Father's desire to flick on the light for you. He is the God who *is* light. He really does want you to be alert to His ways. So the question is not always so much, "What is God telling me to do?" The question may be more, "What do I need to do to clearly hear His voice?"

To hear from Him, you will need to do whatever it takes to be:

- CONSISTENTLY CLEAN. You can't listen to God while clutching your sin. We keep ourselves ready for His ways as we stay cleaned up. The psalmist gives us some direction in Psalm 25:12 (AMP): "Who is the man who reverently fears and worships the Lord? Him shall He teach in the way that he should choose." If we're not reverencing, honoring and worshiping the Lord, we shouldn't be surprised when our communication is interrupted and His ways are difficult to read. Sin is always the biggest obstacle in discerning His will. Sometimes it's the sin of pride—wanting our own way in a situation more than we want to know His. Whatever the sin is, getting rid of it is the first step. We have to confess it and ask Him to clean us up and get us ready to hear.

  Ask the Father if there is anything in your life that might be hindering your understanding of the way He seeks to lead you. At anything He shows you, be ready and willing to embrace His ways and lay those hindrances at the foot of the Cross.

- **PERSISTENT IN PRAYER.** Jesus taught His disciples about not giving up in prayer. In Luke 11 He tells a parable about a man who goes to his neighbor in the middle of the night for bread for his guest. Jesus said, "because of his friend's persistence, he will get up and give him as much as he needs" (Luke 11:8 HCSB). Then Jesus says, "So I say to you, keep asking, and it will be given to you. Keep searching, and you will find. Keep knocking, and the door will be opened to you" (v. 9).

  The more we commune with Him in prayer, the more He is able to get rid of our unclear thinking, the more of His ways He will reveal. Peter gave the reminder to "be earnest and disciplined in your prayers" (1 Peter 4:7 NLT). Have you been seeking an answer but, in essence, not consistently conversing with Him? Ask Him to recharge your prayer life, then do whatever it takes to reconnect with Him in an everyday, heart-to-heart way.

- **BOUND TO THE BIBLE.** We simply can't complain about not hearing from the Father when we haven't bothered reading the letter He's already sent us. God's Word has answers for every need. He will light your way. Psalm 119:105 says, "Your word is a lamp for my feet, a light on my path."

  So many words in that Bible. How can you know which ones are for you? First, know that they all are. Second, remember that His Holy Spirit lives and works inside your heart and mind. He has the power to guide you to the answers you seek if you will stay consistent in getting to know His ways through His Book.

- **PERPETUALLY PATIENT.** Sometimes when we're faced with a question or a situation that seems so urgent to us, we want God to answer in an instant. And sometimes His answers come big and fast—that's always fun. But He often wants to deepen our relationship with Him as we resolutely meet with Him. He delights in every meeting. Don't let your desire for an immediate answer keep you from reveling in His presence as you're seeking Him, delighting in Him, just as He delights in you.

  Do you ever find yourself expecting on-the-spot answers? Are your prayers sometimes more about seeking to be manipulative or demanding rather than seeking the Lord Himself—His will and His ways? The discipline of waiting will build character if you let it. Make sure you're seeking His plan for you and not your own, and then wait patiently for His very best for you. You can be confident in the fact that your answer is coming. John said,

> *Now this is the confidence we have before Him: Whenever we ask anything according to His will, He hears us. And if we know that He hears whatever we ask, we know that we have what we have asked Him for"* (1 John 5:14–15 HCSB).

Mirror, Mirror

What kind of image are you reflecting? Are you making decisions that reflect His ways, His glory? Stay awake! Beautifully alive! Make sure that you're always able to "fog a mirror" spiritually speaking.

Staying resolutely alert to His ways will usher you into a beautiful life and invite peace that will absolutely blow you away. Sleep like a baby, friends, in His glorious peace.

No matter what kind of pillow marks might blow you away in the morning. Because soul-beauty is not really skin-deep at all. Believe it or not, it's not even coffee-deep.

STAYING AWAKE IN HIS WORD

Therefore we do not give up. Even though our outer person is being destroyed, our inner person is being renewed day by day. For our momentary light affliction is producing for us an absolutely incomparable eternal weight of glory. So we do not focus on what is seen, but on what is unseen. For what is seen is temporary, but what is unseen is eternal.

— 2 Corinthians 4:16–18 (HCSB)

DISCUSSION GUIDE FOR
Espresso Your Faith

"AWAKE, MY SOUL!" (PSALM 57:8)

READY TO ROUSE your soul for a faith boost? Would you like to find new ways to live a life of faith that pleases your heavenly Father? Want to understand Him better? His Word can take us there, calling us to attention, alerting us to the things that will grow our faith and cause our relationship with Him to grow closer and sweeter through it all. If you're digging in to this discussion guide for individual personal study time, that's super. A few little tweaks here and there and it will adjust perfectly for simply adding an extra thought or two or alerting to an additional personal application idea. Skip the "Java Jump Start" opener prompts and dive right into the questions for each chapter. There may be a few group-focused questions, but they can be easily adapted to fit your personal reflection time.

Grab your Bible, lift a warm mug of your favorite coffee, and get ready to drink it all in!

DISCUSSION LEADER NOTES

If you're taking a group along for the 30 shots of "faith espresso," this discussion guide can be just the ticket for offering hints and helps as you seek to stay alert to the things we're called to focus on, and for calling others to alertness right along with you. Reading that focuses on the Word of God is always good for giving us a jolt in all the right places. How much more glorious is it when we set a goal that's higher than merely reading the material? Allowing the Lord to energize our faith walk, then watching as He energizes others—even more glorious!

Let's make it a goal to allow the Holy Spirit of God to get personal. To tap us on the shoulder in every place where we need to give attention. As we take those things to heart, we can experience a sweeter faith than ever before.

A chapter a day for 30 days is a great way to lead your group through the 30 "alerts" in one month. You can meet together once a week to discuss the chapters or divide up meetings in whatever way would best fit your group's needs and schedules.

The questions in this guide are personal reflection questions designed to help us think about and fruitfully process what we've seen in God's Word. Each chapter will begin with a "Java Jump Start" discussion kickoff designed to help group members loosen up and, hopefully, will generate a chuckle or two. Sometimes sharing on a surface level can break down barriers and free group members to share on a deeper, more significant level later. As the discussion leader, it's helpful if you have an answer or story ready for the discussion starter, just in case you might need to "open up the opener," so to speak. Shoot for hitting that balance somewhere between sharing enough of yourself to allow your group to trust you, but not so much that you make the discussion too much about you. If you have a close friend or two in the group, it's a great idea to make yourself accountable to them and to ask them to tell you if you're balancing well.

Always make it a goal to be transparent. If you will be real — even if you have a struggle — your group will most often respect your genuineness and they will feel freer to share their own struggles as they come up.

WHAT YOU'LL NEED TO DO EACH WEEK

Encourage your group to read the assigned chapter or chapters before the group meeting, but let them know that even if they get behind in reading, they still won't feel out of place coming to the discussion meetings. Reminders through phone calls or emails are great. You can divvy up those duties or ask one of your group members to be a contact person. Even with a contact person, as group leader, it's great to check in on your group whenever you can. Ask members how you may pray for them. Whether you contact them or not, may I encourage you to make a commitment to pray for each of your group members each week? What life-changing power there is in prayer!

As you're going through the week's assigned reading, make a few notes or observations you would like to point out or comment on during that week's discussion time. If the Lord teaches you something poignant, confronts you on an issue, or deeply moves you in some way, openly share that with your group.

After you've done assigned readings and prayed for your group, look over the discussion questions. Be ready to offer some answers if the discussion needs a little charge, but be careful not to monopolize the chat time.

GUIDELINES FOR DISCUSSION GROUP

You'll want to set up some ground rules for the group from the very first meeting. Here are some suggestions:

- Personal information shared within the group does not leave the group. Remind each other regularly that everyone should be able to share freely and know that no one in the group will ever betray a confidence.
- If someone shares a need or asks for prayer during a meeting, someone should volunteer right then to stop and pray for that need. Just a few sentences will be perfect.
- No cutting remarks or unkind comments to anyone in the group or about anyone outside the group. Uplifting, positive words only.
- Likewise, never correct anyone in front of the group. Belittling or embarrassing someone into changed behavior rarely works. If confrontation needs to happen it should happen in private and be done in love.
- If someone says something contrary to God's Word, however, let her know you respect her opinion, but also let her know in love what the Bible says. His truth needs to be our bottom line on every issue and every group discussion should reflect that.

PRAYERS FOR YOU!

Thank you for taking on the role of discussion group leader. May the Lord richly bless you for your sensitivity and concern for the growth of others and may He bless the entire group in ways you never even saw coming! Could I pray for you?

Heavenly Father, thank You for this child of Yours. Thank You for a willingness of heart to be used by You to touch the hearts of others, by Your grace and for Your glory. What a sweet sacrifice of service. I ask that You would shine special blessings in the group times and in every other place in the leader's life. May the leader come to know the group members in a deeper way, and also know You in deeper ways. Father, I ask that lives would be touched and changed by Your power. I ask that You would work right before the eyes of each discussion leader. I ask that even now You would be bringing in the group members whose lives You can touch through this forum. If there are those who don't know You, Father, please bring them in by Your Holy Spirit. Draw them to Yourself. I ask that You would grant great wisdom for the leader, Your wisdom, and great insight into Your Word. Give leaders that amazing, Jesus kind of sacrificial love for each member of the group. Move and work, oh Lord—all praise and glory to You. In Jesus' name, amen.

Discussion Guide

INTRODUCTION — Perk Up!

Java Jump Start: What's your brew? Do you have a favorite "cool" coffee? What's the weirdest thing you or a family member did to look cool when you were growing up? Any bizarre hairstyles to report? Mullet alerts, anyone?

1. Are you ready for the adventure? Are you willing, as the introduction says, to "consume His instructions" and are you open to seeing how He might strengthen your faith life? How might a person "consume" His instructions? Any idea what that might require of you?

2. Will you take on the challenge offered at the end of the introduction, the challenge to take on the 30 biblical charges to stay alert? Pray now, asking God to let His Word do its work in every little place in your heart.

3. Look at 1 Thessalonians 5:5–11. According to this passage, what are the things that we have as our protection? Think of some practical ways you can use those things to serve the Lord and to build a stronger faith even today. Any new thoughts come to mind about how the Lord might want to apply these truths in your life?

CHAPTER 1: Alert to the Truth — Amazing Glaze

Java Jump Start: What's the funniest things you've ever seen anyone do—or the funniest thing you've done yourself—while in the semiconscious way-too-tired state?

1. According to the definition given in this chapter, what are the three aspects of a rock-solid faith? How would you rate yourself in those three areas?

2. List some of the benefits in life of staying anchored to God's Word. If you're not already studying it every day, will you commit to investing time in His Word every single day for two weeks? What kind of difference does an everyday commitment to reading His Word make in a person's faith life?

3. How can we treasure His Word? Read through the 119th chapter of Psalms. The psalmist is dealing with a lot of difficulty, but God's Word is his rock. Pick your favorite verses from the chapter, write them out, and stick them in your Bible. Let the words be a reminder to you of all that His amazing promises are for us.

CHAPTER 2: Alert to the Eternal — In This World, Not Oven It

Java Jump Start: What's the one household gadget you can't see yourself doing without? Describe a time when you were forced to. Withdrawals maybe?

1. According to this chapter, to be in this world and not of it requires an alertness to what? What do most people pursue and how does the average person look at life? What are some of the world's "shiny things" alluded to in this chapter?

2. On your list of shiny distractions, are there any that you've struggled with? Any that are a distraction to you right now? How do we get rid of them?

3. Look up Romans 12:1–2 in several versions. Choose your favorite and memorize these two verses over the next few days. Let them become part of your thinking—about your thinking.

CHAPTER 3: Alert to the Prayer Connection — Opening a Can of Terms

Java Jump Start: What's the strangest thing you've ever used to open something else? Have any scars from bad "opening" experiences?

1. In the first paragraph under the "Grand Opening" section, can you find several kinds of prayer we're encouraged to be consistent in? (There are seven or eight or so, depending on how you choose to list them.)

2. What does it mean to allow *prayer* to become a "churchy" word? What can we do to keep that from happening? What would it mean to get "extreme" about prayer?

3. Are there any changes you would like to see in your own prayer life? How can you stay more alert?

CHAPTER 4: Alert to a Connection with the Church — Will the Doughnut Be Unbroken?

Java Jump Start: What's the goofiest diet you've seen? Have you tried any weird ones that you'll admit to?

1. What are some practical ways you can apply Hebrews 13:17 in the relationships in your church? On a scale of "burden to joy," how are you doing at supporting and encouraging your spiritual leaders?
2. List the benefits you see of getting involved and staying involved in a good, Bible-believing church.
3. Did you pray the sentence prayer toward the end of the chapter? How can you be intentional about unity in His church?

CHAPTER 5: Alert to Clear Thinking —
O, They Tell Me of an Unclouded Brain

Java Jump Start: What's the most problematic thing you've ever vacuumed up? What's the strangest thing you've ever found when you cleaned out your vacuum cleaner?

1. What should we empty our minds of and how should we do it? Where does prayer fit in? God's Word?
2. Then what should we fill them with? Write out Philippians 4:8–9 in your favorite version and put it in a place you'll see it every day. Let it feed your mind all week. Commit it to memory.
3. When it comes to prayer, do you ever find yourself calling your prayers "faith-filled" when they're actually presumptuously demanding something from the Father? How do we get our prayer time back to communing with Him and delighting in His presence more than focusing on our needs?

CHAPTER 6: Alert to Wisdom — To Every Season, There Is a Thing

Java Jump Start: Any seasonal coffees jump out as your faves? What's the oddest seasonal ritual you've seen?

1. Are there any tough decisions you're facing right now? How can you apply biblical principles to making those decisions? Take time before the Lord about on these things this week.

2. What are three ways this chapter encourages you to seek wisdom? How reliable are they? How do you know?

3. Think about a time you made a choice based on how you "felt" rather than the three ways to seek wisdom you listed in question 2. What happened and what did you learn from it?

CHAPTER 7: Alert to Serving — Coffee Is Served

Java Jump Start: How do you take your coffee? Connect that to how you might describe your personality.

1. Look again at the 2 Peter 1:5–7 passage quoted in this chapter. List all the "add-ins." What's one thing you can do to more consciously pour each of them into your life?

2. First Peter 4:10 says that each of us has received a gift and that we need to use it to serve. List some of the gifts and talents you feel God has given you. How are you using them to serve the Lord and serve His people? Which gives you the most joy?

3. Have you ever seen God equip people for service and even transform their willingness to serve? How was their surrender connected to what He was able to accomplish through them? Are you fully surrendered to Him, too, in the area of your service?

CHAPTER 8: Alert to Sharing Your Faith —
This Just Makes Good Scents

Java Jump Start: What's your fave aroma? How about the "reek-i-est" thing you've ever had to smell?

1. Look at 2 Corinthians 2:14 in this chapter again. How do you think God puts us on display in Christ?

2. Write out the story of how you came to know Jesus and the difference He's made in your life. How can that story affect others?

3. Are there those in your life who need to know Christ? Come up with at least five concrete ways you can be a billboard, putting Christ on display, practical ways you can take on the aroma of Christ.

CHAPTER 9: Alert to Worship — O Magnify — and Liquefy

Java Jump Start: It's so sad when good hair color goes bad. Do you have an entertaining hair-color horror story? Other hair disasters?

1. What does it mean to thirst for the Lord? What are ways you can encourage that thirst? How does He satisfy it?

2. Have you been alert for the presence of God this week? What does a life look like that is lived as a worship-response to the Lord?

3. Commit Deuteronomy 4:29 to memory this week. Let it be a reminder to seek Him with everything you've got. "Seek the LORD your God and you will find him, if you search after him with all your heart and with all your soul" (Deuteronomy 4:29 ESV).

CHAPTER 10: Alert to Loving in His Name — It Is Well with My Role

Java Jump Start: Ever noticed some of those "out there" kinds of warning labels? Like the toilet plunger that came with the warning, "Caution. Do not use near power lines." Share some of your favorites.

1. We're reminded in this chapter that a loving attitude doesn't just happen. It has to be cultivated, encouraged to grow. How can we do that?

2. As we get specific in growing our loving attitude toward others, how does that change the culture in our churches and in our communities?

3. Are you willing to climb underneath the heavy load of a friend? If so, what do you think it could require of you? How might the Lord meet those requirements for you and through you?

CHAPTER 11: Alert to His Coming — What a Way to Go

Java Jump Start: What's the wildest or most wonderful thing you've seen someone do with chocolate? Is there a food you're more passionate about? Maybe some favorite recipes?

1. What effect does it have on a person when life is lived with a constant knowledge that Jesus could come at any moment? Does that describe your life?

2. Is there anything you would do differently today if you knew He was coming tomorrow? How should those thoughts influence your today? Is your life ever more about your own desires, plans, and goals than they are about doing the things God has called you to do? How does remembering that He could come at any moment affect that kind of thinking?

3. How do thoughts of Christ's coming comfort and encourage us? Do you feel that comfort and encouragement?

CHAPTER 12: Alert to the Enemy — Who's Calling the Shots?

Java Jump Start: What is your "comfort drink"? Any favorite add-in to your coffee for a specific frame of mind? Give a rundown of your mood coffees.

1. What is the definition of faith as it's given in this chapter? What difference does faith make in the battle against the devil and his schemes? Name several ways we resist his attacks.

2. Several of the ways the enemy tries to deceive you are listed in this chapter. What are some others? Whatever the deceit, where is our victory?

3. What characterizes a life lived in that victory? Is there a struggle the enemy is using in your life to get your eyes off Christ and to steal away your victory? What are the specific steps you need to take to resist? Will you take them this very day?

CHAPTER 13: Alert to Hope — Hope Springs Internal

Java Jump Start: Kick-start the time with a sense of humor. Your favorite joke or funny story? Bring it.

1. Read Philippians 3:13–14. Have you ever found yourself a little low in the hope department because of a failure or heartbreak of the past? What should a person do to look ahead instead of back?

2. Define hope. Where is yours and how did it get there? How does it stay? How can it grow?

3. According to this chapter, what is the enemy of hope? What does it mean to be "self-sufficient in Christ's sufficiency"?

CHAPTER 14: Alert to Grace — *Venti, Vidi, Vici*

Java Jump Start: List person or not a list person—that is the question. What's the strangest thing you've ever listed? You may want to make a list.

1. Have you ever felt God's grace was not big enough for a sin you've committed? Why is that faulty thinking? What does His grace mean for every sin and every sinner?
2. Look again at the list of three things grace does for us. Is there anything you would like to add to the list?
3. Spend some time today thanking God for His amazing grace. Write out your prayer of thanks to Him.

CHAPTER 15: Alert to Temptation — Tempted and Tried, Keep Wide the Stride

Java Jump Start: Is there something that's a mental trophy of bad shopping choices for you? Something you just had to have then that makes you roll your eyes now?

1. Write down Psalm 1:1 and start committing it to memory. What are the ways we can "keep on walking," not giving in to a temptation?
2. What specific role does God's Word have in overcoming temptation? Are you wielding the weapon of God's Word well?
3. What are some specific ways we can make sure we "don't give the Devil an opportunity" (Ephesians 4:27 HCSB). Is there anything you need to "unplug"? Are you willing?

CHAPTER 16: Alert to the Needs of Others — What Gives?

Java Jump Start: No need to name names, but what's the most bizarre phobia you've ever heard of? Any goofy phobias you would like to admit to?

1. Who has been a role model to you of "looking alive"—staying alert to the needs of others?
2. If loving others and staying alert to their needs is vital, how would you rate your own vital signs? Think of one thing you can do this week to crank up the love another notch.
3. This chapter mentions becoming ready to lay aside our rights, our fears, our possessions, our pride—even our lives—for another

person if we're called to. Are you ready to pray the sentence prayer just before the charge to "look alive"?

CHAPTER 17: Alert to Forgiveness — What's Your Grind?

Java Jump Start: What does your breakfast of choice include? What's the strangest thing you've ever seen anyone have for breakfast?

1. Why do you think harboring bitterness has such a powerful impact on our walk of faith?
2. List the ugly results, addressed in this chapter, that unforgiveness has on our spiritual well-being. Opposite your "unforgiveness" list, add a "forgiveness" side, including what happens in that particular area when a person chooses forgiveness.
3. Is there anyone you haven't forgiven? If not, thank the Lord and ask Him to help you continue in an alertness to forgive. If there is someone, will you commit to making forgiveness a way of life? Go through the steps to forgiveness in the "Let Kindness Truly Win Out" section and let the Lord change your heart.

CHAPTER 18: Alert to a Life Change —
Something to Write Home About

Java Jump Start: If you wrote a book, what would the title be? Would it be action, drama, comedy, or tragedy?

1. Have you received the gift of eternal life through Christ? If you have, tell the story again and rejoice in how different your life is with Jesus than it would've been without Him. Talk about that contrast. Night and day!
2. If you haven't yet given the Lord your life, would you let today make your "night and day" difference? Pray through the "Run Home" steps. Coming to Jesus is the number one most important decision of this life.
3. Whether you're a new believer or a seasoned Christian, are you rejoicing in your story? Are you willing to share it and to commit to be ever-seeking to learn more about your faith life and how to grow in it?

CHAPTER 19: Alert to the Devastation of Sin — Faith That Digs In

Java Jump Start: What's been the most unpleasant surprise you've managed to dig up around your house?

1. Do you ever find those sneaky world philosophies sneaking into your way of thinking, working to convince you that sin isn't really sin? How can you best nip that in the bud?

2. Did you walk through the steps of facing your wickedness? When was the last time you wept over your sin? What happened and what difference did it make in your life? Keep in mind that remembering the cross is waking up to new faith.

3. Will you pray through these questions? *Lord, is there any sin in my life that I've refused to face? *Will You show me and lead me to confess and forsake it? *Will You guide me in doing whatever it takes to keep my life free from sin? *Will You grant me wisdom in making choices that lead me closer to You and farther from sin?

CHAPTER 20: Alert to Expecting the Best — Filled Cup, Chin Up

Java Jump Start: Do you have a beloved calorie-ridiculous food?

1. Do a little self-survey. Keep up with how many times in a day positive words come out of your mouth. How many negative ones? How does your tally look?

2. Are there some negatives in your life? Do you think the Lord might be asking you to see some of those as opportunities for Him to work? How would that change your attitude about them?

3. How are our expectation and our hope tied together?

CHAPTER 21: Alert to Judgment — Half and Half and Half

Java Jump Start: Do you have a selfish indulgence? Something coffee-related? Something chocolate-related maybe?

1. What would the world be like if God didn't judge sin? If nothing was considered sinful, what kind of messes do you think we would find ourselves in right now?

2. Do you think we could truly appreciate His mercy without taking into account His judgment? How does Romans 8:1–4 fit into those thoughts?

3. What should our response be to thoughts of God as Judge? Write out those responses to Him in prayer.

CHAPTER 22: Alert to Perseverance — Is It Live or Is It Mimeograph?

Java Jump Start: Easy button? Coffee button? Or something altogether different? What kind of button would you want?

1. Waiting and persevering seem like opposites. So how do they connect? Can you recount a time when they connected in your life?

2. What happens when a person substitutes perseverance for impatience and aggravation?

3. Paul talked about remaining fit for service by staying "alert and in top condition" in 1 Corinthians 9:26–27. List at least five things you can do to make that happen. Will you plug into those this very week?

CHAPTER 23: Alert to Growing — Only My Barista Knows for Sure

Java Jump Start: Heard of any strange uses for coffee? How about other things around the household — any weird applications you'd like to share?

1. Is there a difference between growing in the knowledge of spiritual things and growing in spiritual things? If so, what?

2. Does your answer to the first question affect the way you live? Does it affect others? Explain.

3. Do you long to see growth in your faith walk? Does that ever become merely wanting to "look spiritual"? How can we tell the difference in our own hearts and how do we keep on "fanning the flames"?

CHAPTER 24: Alert to Staying Faithful in Hard Times — Fall Up, Not Apart

Java Jump Start: Tell about one of your too-many-little-things-falling-apart kind of days.

1. We read in this chapter that there are choices we make every day—choices whether we will trust God and rest in Him or focus on our difficulties. Contrast focusing on the problem with focusing on the "Problem Fixer."

2. Are you able to look for God in the circumstances of daily life? Are you able to rejoice in His presence even when things are falling apart and you don't understand exactly what He's doing? What does it mean to walk by faith during difficult times?

3. Take time to praise Him right now for the work He is doing in your life. Read the James passage again from the "Staying Awake in His Word" section. Can you pray through it, considering the perspective that labels your troubles "a gift"?

CHAPTER 25: Alert to Thankfulness — Thanks a Latte

Java Jump Start: "What do you say?" "Do you think money grows on trees?" "Do you want your eyes to stick like that?" What are some other "parent-isms" you've heard people use to "prompt" their kids?

1. Why do you think thanksgiving is such an important part of worship?

2. Do you think it's important in faith building? Why?

3. Ready to take on "a new appreciation for appreciation" as this chapter challenges us to do? Choose a practical way to live it out in each one of the "E" cues.

CHAPTER 26: Alert to Building Good Character — We Don't Know Beans

Java Jump Start: What's the most dramatic argument you've ever seen someone make?

1. In what ways do you think the Lord is calling you to "represent"?

2. Think of someone who represents you well—in politics, business, or whatever. Why is good character so important in a representative? How does that transfer to how we represent Christ?

3. Have you made it a goal to become transparent? Have you recognized your own brokenness? How does knowing our weaknesses help us in building character and building good reputations?

CHAPTER 27: Alert to Strength — *Coffeetizing* to a Stronger Place
Java Jump Start: What's your coffee forecast for today? Dark with a 50 percent chance of hazelnut? Partly caffeinated with a chance of foam?
1. Is there someone in your life who has been an inspiring example of spiritual strength?
2. How does knowing we have no real strength actually build security?
3. Commit to memorizing Ephesians 6:10–11. Let it remind you every day where strength is, what it is, and what it's not. Praise the God who gives you all the strength you need to "stand."

CHAPTER 28: Alert to Keeping the Faith — Steady as She Grows
Java Jump Start: Anyone else "carb-loading"? What's the most ridiculous "fitness" plan you've seen?
1. How would you define "soul readiness"?
2. Pray through each of the seven "keepers" for keeping the faith in this chapter.
3. Make a plan to apply in a practical way each one of the "keepers" this week — a firm plan that will help you accomplish something of value in each area. Make your plan very specific.

CHAPTER 29: Alert to Discipline — Hot and Cold Running Faith
Java Jump Start: A perpetually warm, perfect cup of coffee. Someone should invent a contraption that will do that. What other devices would you like to see someone invent?
1. How would you define discipline?
2. How do we balance discipline and grace?
3. Look at 2 Corinthians 12:7–10 again. Ready to let the Lord show off His power? Choose right now to give Him your every weakness in prayer.

CHAPTER 30: Alert to God's Ways — Café Before Beauty?
Java Jump Start: What has been your favorite funny moment, listening to others share in the jump starts? What's been the most poignant moment in the study?

1. Has the Lord called you to be alert in an area that particularly stands out for you? Has He shown you anything that surprised you about yourself or about Him?

2. Did you ask yourself the question prompted in this chapter: "What do I need to do to clearly hear His voice?" Which area would you most like to see God work in your life: being consistently clean, persistent in prayer, bound to the Bible or perpetually patient?

3. Will you right now ask Him to call you to alertness in all of those areas and to show you new ways of becoming alert to all He is doing? Spend extra time in prayer, thanking God for His loving work in your life and for all the glorious "alerts" He's given. He is so good!

Get more out of your reading experience with free book club guides, small-group study guides, and more at NewHopeDigital.com.

You Might Enjoy...

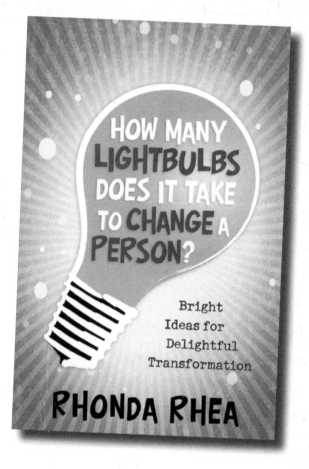

How Many Lightbulbs Does It Take to Change a Person?
Bright Ideas for Delightful Transformation
ISBN-13: 978-1-59669-325-8
N124132 • $14.99

Available in
bookstores everywhere

NEW HOPE
PUBLISHERS
Gospel-Centered. Missions-Driven.

For information about these books or authors,
visit www.NewHopeDigital.com

Use the QR reader on your
smartphone to visit us online at
NewHopeDigital.com

If you've been blessed by this book, we would like to hear your story.
The publisher and author welcome your comments and
suggestions at: newhopereader@wmu.org.